Kim Plunkett

Preliminary Approaches to Language Development

Aarhus University Press

Tryk: Werks Offset, Århus
ISBN 87-7288-001-5

Aarhus Universitetsforlag
Aarhus Universitet
DK-8000   Aarhus C
Denmark

Aarhus Universitetsforlag
Psykologisk serie, 1

Aarhus University Press
Psychology series, 1

Contents

Contents   p.   iii

Preface   v

Acknowledgements   vi

1   Introduction   1
    1.1   Idioms, Metaphors & Translation   1
    1.2   The Organisation of the Book   4

2   Language and Thought   7
    2.1   The Whorf Hypothesis   7
    2.2   Language, Representation and Knowledge   13
    2.3   Language and Communication   23

3   Names, Symbols and Objects   31
    3.1   Names   31
    3.2   Conditions for Naming   32
    3.3   Evidence for Naming   39
    3.4   Explanations of Naming   46
    3.5   Concluding Remarks   53

4   The Linguistic Legacy   55
    4.1   Phrase Structure Grammar   55
    4.2   Transformational Grammar   66

5	**Developmental Psycholinguistics**	77
	5.1 Universal Grammar	77
	5.2 Rules in Child Language	81
	5.3 Pivot Grammars	83
	5.4 Meaning and Context	89
	5.5 A Language Acquisition Device	98
	5.6 Transformational Complexity and Meaning	99
	5.7 Some Problems for a Transformational Description of Child Language	101
6	**Syntax and Meaning Relations in Early Language**	105
	6.1 Case Grammar	105
	6.2 Case Grammar in Child Language	114
	6.3 Meaning Relations	116
	6.4 Word–Order and Propositional Structure	122
7	**Origins of Syntax**	129
	7.1 Traditional Approaches	129
	7.2 Cognitive Development and Syntax Acquisition	132
	7.3 An Interactional Model of Syntax Acquisition	137
	7.4 Concluding Remarks	140
	Bibliography	143
	Index	147

PREFACE

This book discusses two unresolved problems of children's language development. First, how does the child come to the discovery that language can be used as a tool for talking about people, objects, events and relations in the world? Second, how do children come to an understanding of the structure of their native tongue. The first problem is introduced in the context of general approaches to the relationship between language and thought. The discovery that words can be used to name is shown to be related both theoretically and empirically, to the child's developing symbolic capacity. The acquisition of structural linguistic knowledge is discussed in relation to two competing grammatical theories: transformational grammar and case grammar. An introduction to each of these linguistic theories is provided together with an evaluation of their contributions to our understanding of language development. A final chapter discusses alternative developmental mechanisms in the acquisition of language structure.

Acknowledgements

Successive manuscripts of this book were typed with great care and accuracy by Lone Hansen. Her help and encouragement is much appreciated.

CHAPTER ONE

1   INTRODUCTION

1.1   Idioms, Metaphors & Translation

When we speak or write to each other, we often presume that we describe the world as it really is. We presume that our language reflects an underlying reality which everyone can appreciate and
understand. For example, using the sentence "The boy is throwing
the ball", to describe an ongoing event assumes that a particular
situation can be adequately described and communicated by identifying a person performing an action on a given object. The language
that we use seems to have a straightforward link to the idea or
event that we are trying to describe. The different parts of the
sentence have a direct correspondence to the structure of the world
as we perceive it. The sentence describes the world as it is and we
have the utmost confidence that other speakers of our language will
agree with us.

However, the correspondence between the language that we use
and the ideas and events which we thereby try to communicate is not
always so straightforward. "He kicked the bucket", might describe a
male striking a container with his foot but in its idiomatic meaning
the sentence refers to the fact that someone has died. The superficial
form of the sentence again gives the impression of someone performing an action on an object. The underlying reality is somewhat different. Furthermore, we could not decipher the idiomatic meaning of
this expression on the basis of the individual words in the sentence.
Only, a fixed combination of these words can be used to indicate
that a person has died. With **idioms** one either knows the meaning or

1

one does not know. There is no partial understanding. One cannot be sure that the expression used reflects the underlying reality.

There is a half-way house between simple statements of fact that seems to have a direct relation to reality and idiomatic expressions which bear no such relation or, at least, a very unclear relation. A **metaphor** is a word or a phrase used in place of another word or phrase with the purpose of suggesting an analogy or likeness between them. For example, the sentence "The ship ploughs the sea" draws our attention to the similarity between a plough making furrows on the land and a ship's movement through water. To be sure, the use of the term "plough" is not wholly appropriate; a plough normally leaves a permanent furrow whilst a ship does not. However, the metaphor points to a similarity which may lead us to conceive of the ship in a different way. Unlike idioms, we can usually work out or make an educated guess at the meaning of the metaphor. Metaphorical language reflects the underlying structure of reality but often in a way which leads us to re-evaluate our understanding of that reality.

To understand the relation between thought and language we must be aware that there is not always a straightforward connection between what we say and what we mean. "It's cold in here", might very well be a request for someone to close a window or switch on a radiator. Although language is a tool for expressing our thoughts and wishes, a thought can be expressed literally, metaphorically or idiomatically, and each of these three relations between language and thought will affect the way in which the communication is understood. "A volley of oaths" somehow implies more than "a sequence of oaths in quick succession". The metaphor often conjures up nuances which cannot be captured by the literal expression.

As one begins to recognise the different modes of expressing thoughts in language, the notion that literal expressions best reflect objective, underlying reality becomes open to question. The capacity of metaphors to conjure up nuances beyond the capacity of literal expression suggests that language itself has a special role to play in thought processes. The thought underlying a metaphor is no less a thought than one expressed literally. Our thoughts seemed to be shaped just as much by the language we use to express them as by the unconscious from which they mysteriously surface.

2

The notion that language plays a role in the shaping of thought will be readily appreciated by anyone who has attempted to learn and use a second language in a natural setting. The problem of learning a new language is not just one of learning new words and rules for getting those words in the right order. Direct or literal translations from one language to another often fail miserably. There are a number of reasons for such failures. For example, the way objects are classified under a given name varies from one culture to another, rather like the early botanical taxonomies varied in their classification of plants; what we call a "stool" in English may be classified as a "chair" in another language. Idiomatic expressions pose an acute problem in language translations. A literal translation of an idiom will conjure up a completely different understanding from the one intended.

There are subtler problems of translation which seem to pose greater problems for second language learners. We can best illustrate such a problem with a concrete example. In linguistics, a distinction is made between "alienable" and "inalienable" possession. For example, I am said to possess my head, arms, feet, etc., inalienably, but my clothes, books, furniture, etc. are all alienable possessions of mine. Although we can all readily appreciate this distinction, we give no sign that we understand or even pay attention to this distinction in our everyday use of the English language. In contrast, there are languages which must always classify an object according to whether it is alienable or inalienable. For example, one might imagine a pidgin English which talks about "**my** hat" and "**mye** head". We would not be surprised if the speaker of such a language was more sensitive to such differences than speakers of languages which signalled no such distinction. As for the second language learner, not only must he learn the special classification system that the new language uses to name objects and events in the world, but he must also discover what types of classifications are important in the new language. This can be especially difficult if the new language draws upon distinctions which are non-existent in the speaker's native tongue.

Differences between languages have often been associated with differences in national character. French is seen as a sensitive, philosophical tongue whilst German has a stern, authoritarian flavour. If such differences do indeed reflect different underlying conceptions and attitudes towards reality then it is no surprise that inter-cultural communications often break down. A successful communication involves the capacity of a speaker to stimulate a particular mode of thinking in the listener. If the speaker is unaware of how the listener thinks or views the world, his task is made infinitely more difficult. In order to achieve successful communication, the speaker must somehow construct a similar world view as the listener. Learning how to communicate through language is just as much a question of learning about the culture in which one lives as it is learning the rules and the words belonging to a language.

1.2 The Organisation of the Book

In this book, we will consider the process whereby children come to express their thoughts in language. We will concentrate on two aspects of this process. First, how does the child discover that language can be used as a tool for talking about the social and physical world? In particular, how does the young child come to the discovery that objects, people, events and relations have names? Second, we will consider how children learn about the structure of their language. Language structure enables adults to communicate complex ideas and express new ideas in an understandable fashion. How do children master these structures and hence the productive and creative features of language usage?

Chapters two and three take up the general problem of the relationship between language and our conception of the world. Chapter two discusses the approaches which have dominated psychological theorising about language and thought during the past half century. The work of Whorf, Piaget and Vygotsky is briefly introduced and some empirical evidence upon which their theories are based is discussed. Chapter three takes up the more specific problem of how children discover that words can be used as **names** to talk about the world.

Chapters four to seven are concerned with the structure of language and the child's acquisition of that structure. Several grammatical theories are introduced and evaluated in the light of their capacity to help us understand how children acquire language

structure. Chapter four introduces Chomsky's theory of transformational grammar and discusses the results of various psychological
experiments which led to its initial popularity in psychological
circles. Chapter five is concerned with the attempt to use transformational grammar to describe child language. Chapter six presents an
alternative linguistic theory, Fillmore's Case Grammar, that arose
partly as a result of growing dissatisfaction with classical transformational theory. The implications of case grammar for describing
child language are also discussed. Finally, chapter seven discusses
a variety of explanations for the development of language structure
in children.

2   LANGUAGE AND THOUGHT

2.1   The Whorf Hypothesis

In the previous chapter, I argued that the link between reality, as represented in our thoughts, and language is not straightforward. Furthermore, I argued that language is not merely a medium for expressing our thoughts but that it can have an active influence upon the thought process itself. The journey from the unconscious to conscious thought and hence to language is seen as an interactive two-way highway rather than a deterministic, unidirectional process. In this section, we shall consider the views of a man who investigated the active role of language in the traffic of ideas.

Benjamin Lee Whorf lived during the first half of the twentieth century in Hartford, U.S.A. and worked as a fire precaution engineer. It is a tribute to his flexible and active mind that he found time to pursue academic interests which were to have a profound influence on subsequent anthropological, linguistic and psychological research. Whorf's academic bent was that of the comparative linguist and consequently he spent a good deal of his spare time learning and reading about a wide variety of languages of the world, including such diverse examples as Japanese, Hebrew and the Indian languages of his own native America. As a result of his studies, Whorf became convinced that all higher levels of thinking are dependent on language and that the structure of the language one habitually uses influences the manner in which one understands his environment. In the foreword to selected writings of Whorf's work,

Preliminary Approaches to Language Development

Chase provides us with a concise summary of Whorf's view of the role of language in thought.

> There is no one metaphysical view of universal human thought. Speakers of different languages see the Cosmos differently, evaluate it differently, sometimes not by much, sometimes widely. Thinking is relative to the language learned. There are no primitive languages. (Chase, in Whorf, 1956, p. x)

Most of us would probably agree with Whorf that all higher levels of thinking involve "talking it through to ourselves". Even such visual problems as deciding how to reach a destination on the other side of town will involve the names of landmarks and actions-to-be-taken at various points along the route. There can be little doubt that language is an indispensable tool in our thought process-es: A symbolic skill which may be the main cause of mankind's ascendancy over nature and the other creatures on our planet.

However, Whorf's view that speakers of different languages see the Cosmos differently is rather more controversial. Whorf hypothesised that structural differences between languages are of such a nature that they give rise to differing modes of thought in native speakers of the respective languages. We can better understand Whorf's claim by reference to an analogy. A carpenter, in making a piece of furniture or constructing a window frame, has at his disposal a selection of tools with which to accomplish the task. Over the ages, carpenters have refined their range of tools to such an extent that most tasks can be accomplished with relative ease. However, in earlier times one might imagine that certain jobs were rather difficult to perform due to the lack of a suitable tool. Perhaps a particular joint was impossible because the right kind of chisel had not yet been invented. The nature and quality of jobs to be performed were and are dependent on the nature and quality of the tools available. Language is likewise a tool of thought. And just like the carpenter's tools, we would expect the nature and the quality of language to influence the outcome of the thinking process.

Whorf's hypothesis really consists of two inter-related hypotheses. First, it is claimed that there are significant and meaningful, structural differences between the languages of the world. This claim is called the principle of **Linguistic Relativity**. By "significant and meaningful", it is implied that languages are not just copies of each other with the names and word-order rules changed from one language to the next. Our discussion, in the previous chapter, of the problem of making literal translations from one language to another illustrates the kinds of dimensions along which languages can differ from each other in significant and meaningful ways. A good deal of Whorf's own writings is concerned with the task of describing these differences in detail. Secondly, Whorf's hypothesis implies that the language one speaks has a determining influence on the way one thinks. Thus certain modes of thought would not be possible without the presence of particular linguistic structures in one's mother tongue. For example, we conceptualise events like "The boy is throwing the ball" as consisting of actors, actions and objects because these distinctions are inherent in the structure of the language we use to describe the events e.g. Subject-Verb-Object. This aspect of the hypothesis is called the principle of **Linguistic Determinism**. The synthesis of these two principles into the Whorf hypothesis provides us with an exciting perspective on the relationship between language and thought: The medium of thought is so dependent upon and determined by the tool of language that differences in the structure of the tool gives rise to differences in the way the medium is structured.

Stated thus, the argument may seem compelling and obvious. However, the hypothesis should be viewed against the background of an alternative possibility; namely that even though the principles of linguistic relativity and linguistic determinism are correct, the Whorf hypothesis may be wrong. For example, even though languages may differ radically from one another and thought be dependent on the tool of language for its effective operation, the medium of thought may be insensitive to existing linguistic differences so long as it has some language with which to work. To return to our carpentry analogy, the same job may be done by a wide variety of tools provided that each of those tools has the salient property that is necessary for the job. A joint may be cut with a saw or a hammer and chisel. The determining tendency of the symbolic nature of language may be all that is necessary for the medium of thought. I shall call this approach to the relationship between language and thought **Cognitive Determinism** (Schlesinger, 1977).

Preliminary Approaches to Language Development

When considering the Whorf hypothesis, we must take care to evaluate it in the context of the competing hypothesis of Cognitive Determinism. In fact, the two perspectives can be seen as representing opposite views on the relationship between language and thought; the Whorf hypothesis viewing language as a motivating force which gives rise to different modes of thought; cognitive determinism, though accepting language as a necessary and important tool, identifying the thought structuring forces with the individual's perceptual and cognitive experiences, and the biological mechanisms that regulate those experiences.

In a classic study, Carroll and Casagrande (1958) attempted to evaluate the Whorf hypothesis using the methods of experimental psychology. It came to their attention that there lived in a limited geographical area in the state of Arizona, USA, two groups of people speaking radically different languages. Both groups of people belonged to the tribe of Indians called the Navajo. However, one group spoke Navajo as their dominant language; the second group spoke English as their dominant language. In the Navajo language, verbs of handling (such as "to throw", "to pick up", "to drop", etc.) require that the form of the verb be selected according to the **shape** of the object of the verb. Thus, if a Navajo speaker asks another to hand him an object, he must modify the verb form depending on the nature of the object. The verb form used for requesting a long flexible object such as a piece of string differs from that used for a long rigid object such as a stick, and the form differs yet again in asking for a flat flexible material such as paper or cloth. In other words, there is an obligatory linguistic categorisation of objects by shape.

Here we have two groups of people living side by side yet using languages which differ radically in relation to their sensitivity in encoding the shape of handled objects. Carroll and Casagrande hypothesised that Navajo children who speak Navajo as their dominant language should learn to discriminate shape attributes of objects earlier than Navajo children who speak English as their dominant language. The children were presented with ten sets of three objects. The first object in each set served as a model. The children were asked to select the object from the remaining two alternatives that most resembled the model. Consider the set of three objects in Figure 2.1.

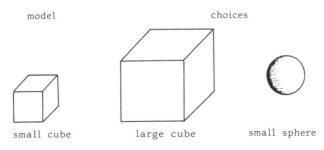

model   choices

small cube   large cube   small sphere

Fig. 2.1.

According to the hypothesis, Navajo-dominant children should select the large cube, because it is the same shape as the model, more often than Navajo children who speak predominantly English. The latter group, mainly speaking a language which does not focus the speaker's attention on shape, should be equally likely to choose either by shape or size, and so would make relatively more choices of the small sphere. Carroll and Casagrande did indeed find that the percentage of shape choices by fifty nine Navajo-dominant children was significantly greater than the percentage of shape choices by the forty three English-dominant subjects on most of the tests. In other words, the Navajo-dominant group was indeed more likely to discriminate on the basis of shape.

In terms of the Whorf hypothesis, this experimental result is of important significance. It supports the notion that thought processes are sensitive to differences in language. In this case, the Navajo language has made shape a more salient attribute for Navajo-dominant children than for English-dominant children. On the basis of this finding, one might expect that English-speaking American children would also be less likely to choose the large cube than Navajo-speaking Navajo children. Carroll and Casagrande performed this additional experiment and found surprisingly that forty seven white, middle-class, English-speaking children from Boston were more likely to select on the basis of shape than the English-speaking Navajo children.

At first glance, this surprising result would seem to cast considerable doubt on the interpretation of the original results in terms of the Whorf hypothesis. Two groups of children, speaking the same language, make their selections according to different principles. Clearly, it cannot be the language that is determining the process of thought in this selection procedure. Carroll and Casagrande point out that the English-speaking American children have considerable practice with form-board toys, i.e. wooden or plastic shapes that have to be fitted into their corresponding holes. In other words, experience has a strong influence on the child's selection.

This interpretation accords well with the perspective of cognitive determinism. However, it is not a refutation of the Whorf hypothesis. The acid test of the Whorf hypothesis is to investigate the role of linguistic differences within a culture rather than across cultures. Otherwise, we cannot control for the factor of experience in our experimental results. Just as cognitive determinism does not deny that language may be an important tool in the effective operation of thought, neither does the Whorf hypothesis deny that experience may have an important influence on thought. The crucial point for the Whorf hypothesis is that the language of a group of people may influence the thought of those people, irrespective of their experiential background. The only way we can investigate this hypothesis is to hold background experience constant whilst we vary linguistic experience. Only then can we be sure that it is the language, not experience, which is influencing the outcomes of our experimental tests. Thus, Carroll and Casagrande's additional experiment with the English-speaking American children was not a test of the Whorf hypothesis because it was an across-culture comparison. However, neither is it entirely clear that Carroll and Casagrande's original experiment comparing Navajo speaking and English-speaking Navajo children was a direct evaluation of the Whorf hypothesis. Despite the fact that the two groups of Navajo Indians live within a limited geographical area, we can be fairly confident that the language differences between the two groups are associated with cultural differences. For example, we would expect that the English speaking group to be more integrated into the western system of values and goals than their Navajo-speaking counterparts. It may be these cultural differences rather than linguistic differences that are responsible for the divergent patterns of categorisation found between the two groups of children.

It has probably become clear that there are profound methodological problems involved in evaluating the respective roles of the Whorf hypothesis (linguistic experience) and Cognitive Determinism (non-linguistic experience) in the development of thought processes. This is because the evaluation of each hypothesis demands the control of a different experimental variable; in the case of cognitive determinism we must hold language constant whilst with the Whorf hypothesis we must hold background experience constant. However, different languages are commonly associated with different geographical areas. Linguistic variations parallel environmental and cultural differences. These parallels exclude the possibility of designing controlled experiments that will enable any clear-cut conclusions to be made about the relative roles of linguistic experience and non-linguistic factors in the development of thought processes.

In normal scientific practice, it is the custom that two competing hypotheses be evaluated in the context of a single decisive experiment. In our present endeavour this procedure is impossible. However, this does not mean that our endeavour is unscientific. Our mistake lies in viewing the two hypotheses as competing with each other. Perhaps a better perspective would be to see the two hypotheses as complementing each other, each having its own influence on the medium of thought, sometimes independently of each other, at other times interactively, as when different languages evolve in response to differing or changing environments. Thus, we need not adopt one hypothesis at the expense of the other. Indeed, the richness of our understanding is increased if we can map out the domains of influence of the two hypotheses. A neglect of either will give us a distorted view of how the child's thought processes are moulded in development and how the child comes to express his thoughts in language.

2.2 Language, Representation and Knowledge

> As I sit at my desk, I know where I am. I see before me a window; beyond that some trees; beyond that the red roofs of the campus of Stanford University; beyond them the trees and roof tops which mark the town of Palo Alto;

beyond them the bare golden hills of the Hamilton Range. I know, however, more than I see. Behind me, although I am not looking in that direction, I know there is a window, and beyond that the little campus of the Center for Advanced Study in the Behavioural Sciences; beyond that the Coast Range; beyond that the Pacific Ocean. (Boulding, 1956).

We do, indeed, know more than we can see. We even know more than we can imagine. Those of us who can ride a bicycle, would find it very difficult to describe the knowledge that we posses relative to those who cannot ride a bicycle. Knowledge is a tricky concept to define, yet we start acquiring it from the day we are born and continue to do so until the day we die. We can also reasonably claim that we are already in the possession of knowledge at the time we are born; the new-born knows instinctively how to search for and suckle his mother's breast; he knows how to grasp objects in his hand; he knows how to cry. However, there is a distinct difference between "knowing how" to perform some activity and consciously "knowing that" I am able to perform that activity because I am in the possession of certain knowledge. Many of us "know how" to ride a bicycle but few of us "know that" we are able to keep our balance by using the centrifugal forces created in always steering a slightly curved path. More often than not, "knowing how" to perform an activity is achieved before we "know that" an activity can be performed in a certain way. The psychologist's goal of understanding human behaviour might be characterised as the attempt to convert a "knowing how" into a "knowing that". In other words, the psychologist often attempts to make explicit the knowledge underlying "how" people are able to do things.

Although the new-born clearly knows how to perform many activities by instinct he is by no means a master of his environment. If left to fend for himself he would certainly die. He must learn a good many new skills before he can literally and metaphorically stand on his own two feet. Learning how to perform a specific skill in adulthood is often aided by direct instruction. An apprentice may learn how to make a piece of furniture by reading about it in a workshop manual or he may learn how to form a particular joint by copying a master carpenter. The young infant is unable to benefit from either of these modes of instruction. He could not understand the language which adults use towards him. Neither could he accurately imitate what the adult does, for he has neither the muscular strength or coordination to succeed. Much of what the six month old knows how to do relative to the new-born, has arisen through the maturation of bodily and nervous processes and the infant's attempts to use these instinctive skills in a trial-and-error fashion in his limited environment.

Piaget, a Swiss psychologist, devoted a good deal of his life to investigating how the infant develops an increasing mastery of his environment. Piaget's work has had a profound influence on developmental psychologists throughout the world. His theorising has also had important implications for educational practise. Piaget's position is of that of the structural interactionalist. He may best be described as a **structuralist** because, unlike his contemporary behaviourists in England and America, he believed that human behaviour and knowledge can best be understood in terms of underlying structures. These underlying structures can be described independently of the particular pieces of behaviour themselves. Thus many different behaviours may be identified as manifesting the same underlying structure. We may illustrate this approach by reference to one of Piaget's best known, though not uncontroversial findings[1].

A preschool child, say four or five years of age, is shown two identical round balls of clay and is asked if they contain the same amount of clay. Typically, the child will answer that indeed they do. One of the balls of clay is now rolled into a cigar shaped object, in full view of the child, and the child asked again whether the two pieces of clay contain the same amount of clay. Surprisingly, the child changes his mind and answers that the two pieces of clay contain different amounts. And, if pressed for further information, will reply that the cigar shaped object contains more clay than the round ball.

Now consider the following scenarios: The same or a similarly aged child is shown two sets of counters arranged in two parallel lines as shown in figure 2.2. below. The child is asked whether the two rows of counters each contain the same number of counters. The

---

[1]   See Brown and Desforges (1979) for a critical review of much of Piaget's work.

child answers correctly that they do. The configuration of counters

```
O    O    O    O    O    O    O
O    O    O    O    O    O    O
```

Fig. 2.2.

is then altered, in full view of the child, so that they resemble the arrangement shown in figure 2.3. below.

```
O     O     O     O     O     O     O
  O  O  O  O  O  O  O
```

Fig. 2.3.

That is, one of the rows is lengthened or shortened with respect to the other. The pre-school child is asked again whether each row contains the same number of counters. This time the child answers that they do not and believes that the more extended row contains more counters.

Piaget argues that the child's understanding of these two "conservations" tasks is governed by the same underlying structures. Piaget describes this structure in terms of what he calls the **Principle of Irreversibility.** Piaget's structuralist approach sees the child's failures as a result of his inappropriate understanding of the two tasks. The child will continue to make similar mistakes on tasks that demand this understanding of which he cannot conceive, until he reorganises the underlying structures which he uses to make sense of the world.

Piaget can be best characterised as an **interactionist** because he believed that the factors influencing the child's changing understanding of his environment have both internal and external sources. The gradual maturation of the child's bodily and nervous capacities sets a constraint on what the child is physically and mentally capable of doing. However, the opportunity to achieve his current potential will depend crucially on the environment in which the child is allowed to practise his capacities. Furthermore, experience in using his new-found skills will stimulate maturational growth and so open up even broader horizons.

Piaget's main goal was to discover the structures underlying human knowledge. He felt he could best undertake this endeavour by studying how children acquire knowledge from their surroundings. In the present context, we are interested in discovering how the development of knowledge might influence the language that a child learns. And similarly, how the language a child learns might influence the development of his knowledge. Piaget (1926) has made some explicit statements about the relationship between language and the development of knowledge. Very briefly, Piaget believed that language itself has only a very minor role to play in the development of knowledge and intellectual development. Characteristically, Piaget sees language as the manifestation of an underlying symbolic skill which the child acquires through experience. This underlying symbolic skill is manifest in other activities such as in the child's play when he pretends that a stick of wood is a telephone receiver or he uses his voice and gestures pretending to be a steam engine. As with cognitive determinism, Piaget did not deny that language may be an important tool in the child's thought processes. However, he did not accept that structural differences between languages could differentially influence the nature of the child's underlying symbolic skills which are themselves the source of the child's linguistic abilities.

Piaget's view of the relation between language and thought is best exemplified by considering his account of the **Sensorimotor period**; the stage in the child's development which begins when the child is born and continues until he is approximately 18 months or 2 years of age. According to Piaget (1945), the child's thought during the sensorimotor period is of such a nature that he is unable to reflect on his own skills and activities. That is not to say that the child is unable to remember events and situations. His familiarity with the sound of a rattle may stimulate him to reach out his arm and shake his hand. To return to a distinction that we drew at the beginning of this section, the sensorimotor child generally "knows how" to perform many activities but he does not "know that" he is able to perform these activities. For example, he is unable to consciously reflect on objects and events in their absence. The thinking of the sensorimotor child is restricted to various forms of interacting with the environment in the "here and now".

It is difficult for adults to appreciate what kind of relationship to the world the child might have if he is unable to imagine or describe his behaviour and the world to himself. Perhaps the best we can do is to consider ourselves performing some skill which we would find difficult to describe to others, like riding a bike or simply walking. The sensorimotor child's thinking reflects an intelligence of perception and action; hence the term sensorimotor.

Piaget argues that the child's thinking will be limited to the "here and now" until he masters the ability to represent objects and events symbolically. A symbol is any entity, concrete or abstract, which can be taken to stand for another object or event in its absence. The relation between a symbol and the thing it stands for can be arbitrary or there may be a similarity between the symbol and the object symbolised. For example, most of the concrete words on this page are arbitrary symbols of the objects for which they stand whilst the piece of wood that a child uses in play as a telephone receiver, while acting as a symbol, has certain physical properties in common with the telephone receiver. Clearly, when a child has mastered the symbolic skill, he has acquired a capacity that is fundamental to many human activities; talking about objects in their absence; being able to imagine things to oneself; to pretend play; to talk about past or future events. Indeed, the very nature of human civilisation is founded upon our symbolic skills. Without our mastery of complex symbol systems we would be unable to communicate the ideas accumulated and developed by our own generation, to subsequent generations. The development of a symbolic capacity is probably the most important single achievement in the evolution of the human species.

For Piaget, the crowning achievement of the sensorimotor period is the child's discovery of the symbol. This is no sudden discovery by the child. Piaget has documented a number of stages through which the child must pass in his development of this capacity. Of particular interest here is how the child comes to know that objects continue to exist even when he cannot see them. This may seem a strange question to ask, but Piaget has uncovered some important aspects of infant behaviour which suggest that when an object is out of the infant's sight it is also out of his mind. Clearly, if one cannot conceive of an object in its absence then the capacity for symbolic representation is also beyond one's grasp. The concept of **object permanence** is indispensable in an adult world where we must plan ahead, taking into acount past events and future possibilities. If we have not mastered the concept of object permanence the world becomes an unpredictable and unstable place in which to live.

During the first few months of his existence, the young infant has very little understanding of the concept of object permanence. When an object disappears from view, it ceases to exist. For example, if a toy falls out of the infant's cot, he will make no attempt to re-establish contact with the object. Or if an object passes too quickly across the infant's field of vision, he will soon give up trying to keep track of it. It simply ceases to exist. The implications of such a view of the child's world are far-reaching. When the mother moves away from the child then she too presumably ceases to exist for the child. Does this mean that the infant experiences a new mother when she returns? I think not. Although the infant cannot conceive of objects in their absence, that does not preclude the infant recognising those objects when they return. The skill of recalling an object for oneself is far more complicated than merely recognising an object. The ability to recognise is a skill embedded in the "here and now". Recall requires a mastery of the symbolic capacity. It is important to remember that the infant's ability to recognise objects functions satisfactorily from a very early age. His ability to recall objects, and thus conceive of them in their absence, requires the ability to reflect on this recognition skill.

The next stage in the development of object permanence suggests that the infant is beginning to conceive of objects in their absence but only if the object moves out of the child's field of vision in the context of an ongoing activity. The classical example given of this type of understanding of object permanence uses a toy train disappearing into a tunnel. At the earlier stage of development, the infant will show surprise when the train reappears from the other end of the tunnel. However, at this later stage, the child's behaviour suggests that he expects the train's reappearance. For example, his eye gaze will move ahead to the opposite end of the tunnel and he will express no surprise when the train re-appears.

Similarly, if an object that the child has been playing with falls out of his cot and disappears from view, he will look over the side of the cot in order to find it. Notice, however, that in each of these cases the child's understanding of object permanence is closely connected to his actions on the object. He will fail to demonstrate such an understanding with objects towards which he is not showing an immediate interest. He will not, for example, attempt to look for objects that he has not been recently actively engaged with and are not in his field of vision.

The second half of his first year, sees the infant making great strides in his understanding of object permanence. He will retrieve objects left in cupboards and other places beyond his vision, as and when he desires them. The infant need not have been recently playing with the object. At first glance, he really does seem to know that objects exist, even when he cannot see them. However, consider the following situation: The infant is sat in front of two screens A and B. They may be cushions, covers or vertical pieces of wood. The important thing is that an object can be hidden under or behind the screen. A toy which the child likes playing with is shown to the child and then, in full view, hidden behind screen A. This proce-dure is repeated several times and each time the child retrieves the object. On the third or fourth hiding, the toy is hidden, in full view of the child, behind screen B. Surprisingly, the child continues to search behind screen A even though he has seen it hidden behind screen B. If the procedure is repeated several times, the child con-tinues to look behind screen A. This error is known as the "Stage 4 error" because it is characteristic of children in the fourth of Pia-get's six stages that trace the development of object permanence. Such an error does not suggest the behaviour of an individual who has a full understanding of object permanence. Indeed, it would seem that the 8 or 9 month old infant considers objects to exist only in particular places or locations rather than having an independent existence of their own. These object locations would seem to be placed where the child normally finds the object in the course of his day-to-day activities. The concept of the object is thus still closely tied to the child's own actions on the world. Objects only exist relative to the child's own activities. They do not exist in their own right.

The stage 5 child knows that he must often search for objects where they have not been found before. Thus, in the screen test he will search behind either screen A or B depending upon where he saw the object hidden. Yet the stage 5'er continues to make a type of error which we would not consider typical of an individual who has grasped the concept of object permanence. Suppose that the object which has been hidden behind screen A, is moved from behind screen A to screen B in such a way that the object is hidden in the hand of the hidder so that the child cannot see the object. This procedure contrasts to previous ones where the child has always had a full view of the object when it is not hidden behind one screen or the other. Although the stage 5'er is able to retrieve the object from behind screen B when he sees it hidden there, in this new situation he makes no attempt to search for the object behind screen B. Instead, the child concentrates exclusively on screen A, the location where he last saw the object. The child seems unable to conceive of the object undergoing invisible displacements. That is, he is willing to accept that the object can exist in different places but only provided he has seen the object in those places already.

The ability to conceive that an object has been moved to a new location requires that the child understands that others can perform actions on the object that change its location. That is to say, the object must exist independently of his own actions and of particular locations. The child must be able to imagine or conceive of an object being moved about by others. Being thus able to conceive of an object in its absence, and not tied to his own actions, the child will be able to imagine its existence in a variety of places and hence predict its new location. The stage 6 child is thus able to search behind screen B, after an invisible displacement, and hence successfully retrieve the object.

To be able to conceive of an object in its absence and imagine various actions being performed on the absent object, clearly involves the symbolic capacity to mentally represent an object and mentally manipulate that representation. The sixth stage of object permanence thus heralds the child's mastery of the symbolic capacity. He is approximately 18 months to 2 years old. The young child's new-found ability to symbolically represent objects and events in his mind enables him to finally escape the world of the "here and now" that imprisons the sensorimotor child. At long last the child cannot only "know how", he can also "know that". For example, he can "know that", if he wishes to obtain an object that is out of reach he can either go and get the object or use some tool to reach out and retrieve the object. He "knows that" this is possible without actually having to perform the action because he can symbolically represent the event to himself, as if he were performing a mental experiment. Children at an earlier stage of development would "know how" to retrieve the object but they would not "know that" they were able independently of performing the action. This new-found capacity for symbolic representation enables the child to reflect on all his "knowing how" knowledge and use it to much greater effect.

An understanding of how the child develops a concept of object permanence is important for at least 2 reasons. First, knowing that objects exist and things can happen independently of our own interaction with them is an important prerequisite for many aspects of our knowledge. For example, our ability to predict future events in the world is dependent upon our ability to construct a model of the world in our minds. This model is not a miniature copy of the outside world but an abstract representation of all our accumulated knowledge. Neither is this model a static structure. It is a model that is able to change itself through the process of self-reflection. And because it is not limited to the "here and now", we are able to fantasise about future and possible worlds and so begin the process of transforming fantasy into reality. If Piaget is correct in claiming that the young infant does not yet possess this capacity for self-reflection, and his object permanence studies have been replicated with many different children in many different cultures, then our investigation of the developmental relationship between language and thought must contend with its serious implications. Language is a symbolic skill par excellence. For example, naming an object in its absence implies an understanding of the independent and permanent existence of that object. One might therefore expect that the ability to name an object in its absence will not emerge until he has reached the sixth level of object permanence. We shall return to this very issue in the next chapter.

However, there is an even more fundamental issue that needs to be raised here. If the sensorimotor child's medium of thought is pre-symbolic then it is difficult to see how language as a symbolic skill could have any influence on the sensorimotor child's intellectual development. Language as a symbolic skill must be completely unknown to the sensorimotor child. Thus, if Piaget is correct in his claims, we must consider children during their first two years of life to be pre-linguistic beings. It is in this context, that we should evaluate Piaget's statement that language is secondary to thought. Indeed, we can see that from this perspective it is impossible for language to emerge before the necessary intellectual (symbolic) skills are mastered.

In this way, language builds upon the foundations of thought and has precious little influence on the development of those foundations. Furthermore, since the child's intellectual development (according to Piaget) is determined by the interaction of maturational and environmental factors, we must conclude that the perspective of cognitive determinism best describes the development of thought during the early years of life. From a Piagetian perspective, the Whorf hypothesis is simply irrelevant.

2.3 Language and Communication

So far in this chapter, we have considered two distinct perspectives on the relationship between language and thought. We now turn to a third approach which in some ways can be seen as a middle road between the Piagetian and Whorfian perspectives, though it too has its own distinct flavour. This third approach was first expounded by the Russian psychologist Vygotsky.

Unlike Piaget, Vygotsky believed that language plays a crucial role in the development of thought:

> Thought development is determined by language, i.e. by the linguistic tools of thought and by the sociocultural experience of the child ...... The child's intellectual growth is contingent on his mastery of the social means of thought, that is, language (Vygotsky, 1962, p. 51).

Such statements as these would appear to set Vygotsky fair and squarely on the side of the Whorf hypothesis. However, such a conclusion would be an insensitive interpretation of Vygotsky's position. In pointing to "the linguistic tools of thought" it is unclear whether Vygotsky believed that structural differences between languages can affect the operation of the medium of thought, and in referring to "sociocultural experience" it is clear that Vygotsky acknowledged the role of non-linguistic factors in the development of thought. For Vygotsky, a theoretical perspective which treats language and thought as two separate entities will certainly fail to capture the unique properties which are the result of their interaction. Vygotsky illustrates his position by reference to a vivid analogy. He sees a study of the development of language and thought which treats them as independent and separate as like the chemist who attempts to explain the properties of water in terms of the properties of its component elements, hydrogen and oxygen. Clearly, the attempt breaks down. Consequently, Vygotsky believed that an understanding of the relationship between language and thought can only be gained by studying phenomena where the two meet together. A clear example of the meeting of language and thought can be identified in Verbal Thought; the process in which our inner thoughts take on the cloak of language without them necessarily being expressed overtly. Vygotsky argued that the smallest unit of analysis that contains the essential properties of the interaction between language and thought can be found in **word meaning.** By studying the meanings that adults and children use for their words, we simultaneously gain access to the thought and the language. For meaning is the bridge between the two; the bridge by which language and thought can mutually influence each other.

However, in identifying word meaning as the central unit of analysis in the study of language and thought, Vygotsky did not imply that the relationship between them is held constant by this bonding bridge:

> The most important fact uncovered through the genetic study of thought and speech is that their relationship undergoes many changes. Progress in thought and progress in speech are not parallel. Their two growth curves cross and recross. They may straighten out and

run side by side, even merge for a time, but they always diverge again. (Vygotsky, 1962, p. 33).

The combination of language and thought in word meaning marks the first time in which their paths of progress meet. Like Piaget, Vygotsky believed that there is a pre-linguistic phase in the development of the child's thought processes. That is to say, during the first stages of development, the child's thought is uninfluenced by and independent from his linguistic development. However, unlike Piaget, Vygotsky believed that there exists a pre-intellectual phase of speech development. That is, language begins to develop before it is used in combination with the child's intellect. Vygotsky saw language during its pre-intellectual phase as fulfilling principly a social function. The infant uses language for communicating desires and wishes and not for the communication of word meanings which must await the synthesis of language and thought. In this stage of language development, the child uses his cries and whines in combination with gestures to maintain a communicative channel with his listeners. No meanings are conveyed. During this period, language and thought are following their own paths of development. However, around the age of 2 years (note that this is about the same time that Piaget estimates the child as acquiring the symbolic capacity), the paths of language and thought converge and the synthesis that results in the creation of word meaning occurs. In terms of the child's behaviour, we observe a sudden growth in the child's vocabulary as a result of his sudden, active curiosity about words in asking, "What's that?".

In contrast to both Whorf and Piaget, Vygotsky sees neither language nor thought as having a relationship of dominance over the other. Their relationship is one of a synthesis to create a new way of understanding and interacting in the world. Language and thought are both changed as a result of this synthesis. Language, which begins as a medium for social expression, takes on the role of expressing ideas or meanings. Thought, which was an internal individual experience, can now be communicated to others and correspondingly influenced by others through the medium of language. The need to express one's individual, idiosyncratic thoughts together with the need to make these thoughts communicable enforces on the child a discipline which can only be realised in the creation of word meanings. Indeed, Vygotsky argues that the internalisation of language through the creation of word meanings is one of the principles mechanisms of socialisation of the child into his native culture.

Vygotsky presents us with a case study of how word meanings change through the course of development. It is a forerunner of many modern day studies of concept formation and the implication of its results, a number of which Vygotsky failed to realise, are only just beginning to have their impact on present day understanding of child development (Bowerman, 1978). Vygotsky wanted to investigate the role of language in the process of concept formation. In accordance with his theoretical biases, he decided that the best way to proceed was to study the development of word meaning. Vygotsky assumed that word meanings presented the key to the structure of our concepts. Therefore by studying word meanings he could discover how the structure of concepts developed over time.

The advantage of using word meanings to investigate concepts is that we use words to communicate ideas. In order to communicate effectively, the words we use must have stability in their meaning and consequently in the concepts to which they refer. If the meaning of a word changed each time we used the word, communication would break down pretty quickly. Thus, we might investigate concept formation by studying how word meanings are defined; by asking the child, for example, how he defines the words that he uses. However, Vygotsky criticised this approach on the grounds that any definitions provided may reflect the child's general and linguistic knowledge rather than the word meaning or concept itself. Furthermore, studying the definition of word meanings tells us nothing about how those definitions were arrived at. We are only studying the finished product and neglecting the developmental process which was the original aim.

Instead, Vygotsky argued for an experimental study of concept formation which avoids the problem of pre-defined words and idiosyncratic experience. He used what have become known in the literature as Vygotsky's blocks. They consist of 22 wooden blocks varying in colours, 6 different shapes, 2 heights (the tall blocks and the flat blocks), and 2 sizes of the horizontal surface (large and small). On the underside of each figure which is not seen by the subject, is written one of the four nonsense words: "lag", "bik", "mur", "cev". Regardless of colour or shape, "lag" is written on all tall large figures, "bik" on all flat large figures, "mur" on the tall small ones, and "cev" on the flat small ones: The subject's task is to identify which blocks belong to each of the 4 concepts. The experimenter presents the task to the subject in the following way: One of the blocks is removed from the collection which lies before the subject in a haphazard fashion. The subject is then shown the name of the sample block and asked to select from the remaining blocks those which might have the same name. After the subject has made a selection, the experimenter makes a record of the blocks selected. If the selection includes examples which do not belong to the same category as the original block, the experimenter indicates to the subject that one of his choices was wrong by showing him the name on the incorrect choice. All the blocks are then returned to the collection, except those whose names have been revealed, and the subject asked to make another selection of blocks which might have the same name as the original block. The process continues until the subject has "discovered" the concepts, i.e. he can define them for himself, or there are no more blocks left unturned.

This experimental approach to studying concept formation enables one to investigate the ongoing process in terms of the subject's selection of blocks and the comments he makes in reflecting on his judgements. Because the experiment uses artificial concepts which the subject has never used before, the complete process of concept learning can be studied from beginning to end. Vygotsky and his colleagues performed this experiment on both children and adults, as well as a number of handicapped groups. Here we shall concentrate on the developmental differences he found between children and adults. However, before considering the precise nature of the results that Vygotsky found, it is worth emphasising the following two points. First, Vygotsky assumed that the results obtained in studying the emergent meanings of the four nonsense words reflect the development of word meanings in everyday language. Secondly, Vygotsky believed that true concepts could be defined in terms of a set of attributes such that every member of the concept shared this set of defining attributes. If an object possessed all these defining attributes then it is automatically a member of the concept. However, if an object lacks even one defining attribute, it cannot be considered a member of the concept. The nature of the materials used by Vygotsky fitted ideally to investigating the development of concepts of this type.

Vygotsky describes three distinct ways of solving the blocks task. Each way corresponds to a particular stage in development. During the first phase, say $3\frac{1}{2}$ years to 7 years, children seem to select blocks from the remaining collection on an arbitrary or, at least, idiosyncratic basis. For example, the child may select the first block he looks at or the one closest to him. He does not seem to select blocks on the basis of their relation to the original block. Vygotsky calls this the trial-and-error phase. The selection is made at random and each block added is a mere guess or trial.

The next phase Vygotsky calls the stage of thinking in complexes. We can distinguish two important sub-stages in this period. First of all, the child selects blocks on the basis of a relationship to the original block. For example, a block may share the same shape or colour or both. However, the basis for selection varies from one block to the next so that subsequent blocks, though sharing features in common with the original block do not necessarily have anything in common with each other. These are called **associative complexes**. An alternative type of complex is called a **collection**. The child picks out objects differing from the sample in colour, in shape, in size, or in some other characteristic. He does not pick at random, however. He choses them because they contrast with and complement the other attributes of the sample which he takes to be the basis of the complex. The result is a collection of the colours or shapes present in the experimental material, e.g., a selection of blocks each of a different colour. Vygotsky draws our attention to the occurrence of collection-like structures in everyday life, e.g., cup, saucer and spoon or shoes and socks. The child's experience of these real-life associations apparently leaves its mark on underlying processes of concept formation.

In the final phase which occurs sometime after puberty, the adolescent uses a true conceptual structure to make his selections. That is, he uses an abstract generalisation based on the dimensions used to characterise the blocks. When a mistake is made, a careful consideration of the mistaken block's relation to the original block enables the adolescent to eliminate the irrelevant dimensions and so quickly come to a solution of the problem. Vygotsky regards this way of defining word meanings and so structuring concepts as the highest level of logical behaviour attained in development. However, Vygotsky does not deny that more primitive levels of conceptual definitions exist in adulthood. Associative complexes seem to underlie the meaning of some adult words. For example, all the people designated by a single family-name are not members of that group because they possess the same set of defining attributes. On the contrary, they are likely to share very few attributes with each other. They are grouped together under the same "concept" because of their varying relationship to one or two nuclear members of the group. In fact, there is an abundance in both adult and child language of words meanings which can be defined in terms of associative complexes (Rosch, 1975).

Our description of Vygotsky's experimental investigation of the process of concept formation only skims the surface of the extensive studies that he carried out. However, it will serve to illustrate a number of important features of Vygotsky's work. First, it is clear that the nature of the concepts underlying the words we use, change during the course of development. Thus, even though a child may use the same word as an adult and use that word to name the same object, say a dog (if we accept Vygotsky's findings as being applicable to naturally-defined words), then we must conclude that in many cases the underlying meanings will differ radically from adult to child. Secondly, I argued earlier in this chapter that we could view the relationship between language and thought in terms of two alternative hypotheses, cognitive determinism and the Whorf hypothesis. Vygotsky brings to our attention that we should not attempt to see the relationship just in terms of one or another hypothesis. Just as the very nature of word meanings change in the course of development so does the nature of the relationship between language and thought. Thus any single hypothesis is unlikely to be correct. Finally, Vygotsky points out the importance of the social nature of the developmental process. Thus, structures like collection complexes would seem to underlie many of our culturally bound word meanings. The child's affinity for creating such structures in his thought may be fundamental in his becoming a member of the social community.

They enable him to identify with modes of categorisation which are exclusive to his own culture.

CHAPTER THREE

3   NAMES, SYMBOLS AND OBJECTS

3.1   Names

Traditionally, the course of language development has been measured
in terms of the child's vocabulary growth. A wealth of diary studies
by parent academics, document the range of adult-like words that
children have at their command during the early period of language
development (see Clark, 1973, for a review). Alternatively, cross-
sectional studies have attempted to estimate the size of a child's
vocabulary through the use of comprehension techniques, such as re-
sponding to an instruction to pick out a named toy from a pile of
different toys. Whatever the method used, the assumption has most
often been that children are learning a catalogue of **names**. The
names may be about objects in the world - "daddy", "dog" and
"car", or they may describe actions which are common in the child's
environment - "give" or "sit", "pick" or "kick". In either case,
adults generally assume that the child uses the word **as a name to
refer to** a particular object or action.

Knowing that objects and actions can be named is an important
part of knowing one's native language. Indeed, naming is such an
essential part of language that it might seem impossible to imagine a
language that does not make use of names in some way or other.
When adults assume that a child is using a word as a name to refer
to an object or action, they are reflecting on their own naming
skills and interpreting the child accordingly. For example, when a
15 month old child utters the word "wow wow" at the sight of a toy
dog, most adults will interpret this behaviour as the child naming
the object either for himself or the adult. The concept of naming is

so ingrained in our own linguistic behaviour that it is difficult to imagine that the child might not be engaging in a similar process.

It is instructive to ask when and how children learn that objects and actions have names. It is, of course, possible that naming is not a skill that children have to acquire. Naming may be a human capacity that awaits only an adequate maturation of the child's phonetic skills for its concrete manifestation. The concept of naming may be part of the child's inherited mental apparatus. The act of naming awaits only the right linguistic conditions, i.e. adequate phonetic development and exposure to names. On this view, the child's very first words are potentially names. On the other hand, the capacity to name may be a skill that the child has to learn, over and above learning the sounds appropriate to his own native tongue. If the child has not developed this capacity by the time he has mastered his first words, then clearly we should not interpret these first utterances as acts of naming.

The question as to whether the concept of naming is a capacity possessed by the child before he manifests language or whether it is a capacity that itself must be acquired during the course of language development is important because it has implications for our understanding of the role of naming in the acquisition of linguistic knowledge. I speculated earlier that it might seem impossible to imagine a language that does not make use of names. The capacity to name may be an essential prerequisite for the emergence of language. On the other hand, if the child has not developed the capacity to name objects and actions by the time he utters his first words, then we need to consider what status we should attribute to these earliest words. If they are not names, then what are they? Furthermore, we need to consider how the child discovers that things have names. For example, does the child make this discovery through his experience with language? Or does the child discover the concept of naming through some other non-linguistic social or cognitive experience?

3.2   Conditions for Naming

To a great extent, the answers to these questions depend upon one's understanding of the concept of naming. What does it mean to say that an object has a name? As adults, we use names as a means for **referring to** or **identifying** objects or actions. A name may refer to a unique individual, as in the case of proper names - "John", or it may identify an object as belonging to a class of objects, as in the case of common names - "flower". Names may refer to objects or actions which are either concrete or abstract; "Hell" vs. "New York" or "think" vs. "kick". And just as a common name can be used for a variety of objects, so can a single object have a variety of names. For example, the family pet may be called "a dog", "an animal", or just plain "Fido". Names are used continuously in language for an enormous variety of things and for an equal variety of purposes. You might like to contemplate how one decides to name the family pet on different occasions. When is he called "the dog" rather than "Fido"?

Irrespective of the particular object or action named or the reason for naming it, all acts of naming share certain fundamental properties. When a speaker performs the act of naming, he makes a connection between a spoken word and a particular object or action. At the risk of over-simplification, we might imagine that this process consists of three distinct components; the word or phrase used to perform the act of naming; the object or action named; and a connecting link between these two previously mentioned components. Figure 3.1. summarises this description.

Fig. 3.1.

Normally, we would say that the connecting link component represents the **symbolic** relation between the word or phrase used to name and the object or action named. However, in order not to prejudge the issue of what is involved in naming, will use the more neutral term "connecting link".

Preliminary Approaches to Language Development

This brief analysis of the act of naming, gives us some hints as to what skills the child must possess before he can begin to name. For example, it is clear that to name an object, the child must have a sufficiently well developed phonetic system for him to produce recognisable words. In normal children, this condition is fulfilled towards the end of the first year. Deaf children do not make such fast progress. Nevertheless, they could in principle fulfil this condition by demonstrating a sufficient mastery of sign language. It is often emphasised that a name should have an arbitrary relation to the object or event being referred to by name. Using a word like "wow-wow" to refer to a dog does not fulfil this condition. The use of an arbitrary sign encourages the interpretation that the child is engaged in the act of referring and is not merely imitating or pointing at some property of the object concerned. In the absence of other behavioural criteria, the condition of arbitrariness is a useful guideline for establishing whether a child has learnt to refer. However, using a word like "wow-wow" does not exclude the possibility that the child conceives of it as a name for dogs. Indeed, children continue to use such labels long after it is abundantly clear that they have discovered that objects and events can be referred to by name. Thus, arbitrariness of signs must be considered a conservative criterion for establishing the presence of naming, especially if other behavioural evidence can be martialled to demonstrate that children have already mastered this skill.

A second component necessarily involved in the act of naming is the object or action itself. Naming, without referring to something or someone, is simply not naming. It is the utterance of empty sounds. At first glance, the object component of naming would seem to be fulfilled without any effort whatsoever on behalf of the child. Unless one is committed to some extreme form of idealism, most of us would agree that "out there" is a physical world made up of objects, both moving and stationary. For the young child, the possibility of having objects to name is fulfilled by the very nature of the world in which he lives. He is surrounded by objects to which he can give names. However, you will recall our discussion in chapter two (p. 17-23) of Piaget's (1945) view that young children, during the first two years of life, do not have a fully developed concept of object permanence. In chapter two, I described a number of studies by

Piaget which suggest that when an object is out of an infant's sight or grasp, then that object ceases to exist for him. Furthermore, early developments in the concept of object permanence suggest that it is the infant's own activities which endow the object with an existential quality for the child, e.g. using the object for a particular purpose or regularly finding it in a special place. In any event, Piaget claims that young children do not have a conception of the independent existence of objects and actions until the end of the sensorimotor period (normally the end of the second year).

Piaget's theory of the development of object permanence would seem to have important implications for our understanding of how children learn to name objects and actions. If a child does not have a concept of the stable and independent existence of objects, then it is unclear how the child could come to reliably and consistently name those objects. If the act of naming necessarily involves an object (or some representation of that object e.g. a concept) and the child has not yet developed an object concept, then it is difficult to see how he could come to name anything. In fact, the logic of the argument leads us to conclude that the act of naming should not be mastered by the child until the end of the sensorimotor period: Naming involves the conceived existence of the named object. If a child has not yet developed such a conception then the act of naming cannot be mastered. The onset of object permanence, like the development of adequate phonetic skills, would appear to be a necessary condition for learning how to name.

A brief review of the literature on the relation between children's cognitive development and their language development reveals some evidence for the prediction that the attainment of object permanence is a necessary prerequisite for naming. Bloom (1973) found that her daughter Alison did not use names for objects reliably and consistently until she had reached sensorimotor stage 6. At the same time, 1;6 (year; month), Bloom also found a sudden increase in Alison's naming behaviour. Since sensorimotor stage 6 includes the achievement of object permanence, Bloom's findings support the notion that object permanence is a necessary prerequisite for naming. However, Bloom did not include an independent measure of object permanence in her study of Alison. Her assessment of Alison's cognitive level was based on a general evaluation of Alison's behavioural skills.

A more careful study of the relationship between object permanence and language development was carried out by Corrigan (1978). Corrigan studied three children throughout their second year. She made observations of the children's level of object permanence as measured by the Uzgiris-Hunt (1975) infant assessment scales and compared this to data she collected on the length of the children's utterances and their rate of vocabulary growth. You will recall from chapter two (p. 17-23) that attainment of object permanence is not an all-or-none affair. Children pass through a series of six stages, the final stage culminating in the achievement of the concept of an independent, existing object. During the year of the study, Corrigan charted the children's development through these stages, on each visit assigning a child to a particular level. In fact, Corrigan found it necessary to divide individual stages up into sub-stages. In this way, gradual changes within a stage in the child's understanding of object permanence, could be distinguished. All in all, Corrigan specified 21 different levels through which the child must pass for the attainment of full object permanence. Thus, for example, level 15 represented the beginning of stage 6 while level 21 represented the final achievement of object permanence.

Although Corrigan found no direct correlation between the children's level of object permanence and the length of their utterances, i.e. she could not predict an individual child's level of object permanence from a knowledge of the length of his utterance or vice versa, she did find that the greatest increases in vocabulary growth did not occur until or after the time each child had reached level 21 of object permanence i.e. not until full object permanence had been achieved. To the extent that the increases in vocabulary growth reflect increases in the child's repetoire of names and naming behaviour, the attainment of object permanence would seem to be associated with the act of naming.

I have argued that object permanence should be important for naming because to name an object the child must be able to conceive of the existence of the object. This seemingly simple and necessary condition would appear to account for the fact that vocabulary development does not really "take off" until the full attainment of object permanence.

However, level 21 of Corrigan's object permanence scale requires the child to solve the problem of finding an object after it has been invisibly displaced under three consecutive screens. That is, the child must be able to conceptualise the existence of an object when he cannot see it and imagine that it can change location without he himself acting on it. In the discussion of the role of the object concept for the act of naming, I did not claim that naming necessarily involves the ability to refer to an object in its absence. The important and necessary condition for **naming** is that the child understands that the object exists as an entity distinct from other objects and that there is a world "out there" distinct from his own thoughts and sensations. The child's ability to find objects hidden behind screens as early as stages 4 and 5 would strongly suggest that he has already developed a fairly mature concept of an objective world, even though he may not be able to conceive of that world in its absence. It seems reasonable to assume that provided the child can conceive of the existence of objects, **even if they must be in his immediate perception,** then the necessary level of object permanence has been fulfilled as far as the act of naming is concerned. In other words, level 21 or stage 6 of object permanence need not be achieved for the act of naming to occur. The necessary object concept conditions are achieved at least as early as stage 4.

In the discussion of her results, Corrigan provides us with an important piece of evidence which suggests that level 21 (the end of stage 6) of object permanence is not a necessary prerequisite for the act of naming:

> At the onset of stage 6 (level 15), the child speaks only about objects that are present, so that he does not have to coordinate his action of saying a word with a representation of an absent object. This is still an advance over stage 5, where he produces words that are imitations of an adult model, or words that become attached to his action schemes. (Corrigan, 1978, p. 187).

In this extract, Corrigan makes it quite clear that her three subjects were using words to talk about objects as early as level 15 (the onset of stage 15). In real terms, this means that the children were talking about objects which were present in their environment at least 6 months before they achieved full object permanence. This is a relatively early accomplishment when one considers that object permanence was achieved by 18 months for 2 of the 3 children and by 20 months for the final child. It is worth pointing out that none of the children had more than 2 words in their vocabulary by the time they achieved level 15 of object permanence. Thus, Corrigan's claim that her children are using words to talk about objects is based on very little data.

However, of more importance in the present context is our interpretation of Corrigan's phrase "... the child speaks only about objects that are present, ..." Are we to assume that "speaking about objects" is the same as naming an object? If a 5 month old child approaches his mother with outstreched arms as if wanting to be picked up and says "Mum!", should we interpret this speech act as an act of naming? Unfortunately, the answer is not at all clear. The child might be referring to or naming his mother. Alternatively, he might be using a word that is effective in getting his wishes fulfilled, without any conception that the word is or could be a label for his mother. Indeed, here lies the crux of the problem of understanding how children learn the act of naming.

As I pointed out earlier in this chapter, naming entails a connecting link between the word or phrase used to name and the object or action that is named. However, this connecting link would seem to be of a special kind. Contrary to many behaviourist interpretations, it is unlikely to be a simple association between a word and an object. The object of reference in the case of the personal pronouns "I" and "You" shifts so rapidly even within a single conversational setting that an explanation of naming as the conditioned utterance of a word to the presence of a particular object is simply inadequate. If "I" or "You" were interpreted as referring to one and only one individual, then many conversations would become hopelessly lost:

> I wouldn't do that if I were you.
> No! But I am not you, am I?

The meaning of "I" and "You" depends upon who is doing the speaking. The speaker must learn that "I" can refer to people other than himself and that "You" can sometimes refer to himself as well as his listener. The inflexibility of behaviouristic, associationist accounts of naming where word and object are rigidly bound together, makes them unsuitable for explaining a phenomenon of behaviour which demands such a high sensitivity to the context of use of words. The connecting link involved in the act at naming would appear to be the very realisation that objects can be named and that they have names.

I give this rather tautologous description partly as a cover up for our not knowing what it really means when we say an object has a name but more importantly because it is clear that discovering that objects can be named is an important part of a child's intellectual and linguistic development. I reduced the acts of naming to three component parts; the word, the object, and the connecting link. We have discussed how the word and the object components might prevent the child from performing the act of naming. We can tentatively conclude that they should not, in themselves, prevent the child from naming objects with his very first words. However, we now see that there is a further constraint i.e. given that a child can produce words and has a sufficiently well developed object concept how does the child discover that words can be used to **name** objects.

3.3   Evidence for Naming

How does the child come to construct a connecting link between a word and an object in such a way that he conceptualises the relationship as one of naming? In asking this question I do not mean to imply that in order to name objects, the child must have some explicit philosophical conception of what it means to name objects. Indeed, that is part of the task we are trying to achieve in this chapter. Rather, we may ask the question as to how the child comes to have the expectation that objects have names and how might we as developmental psycholinguists come to recognise that the child has this expectation? The second part of the question is probably easier to provide an answer to than the first part.

We might recognise that young children have developed the expectation that objects have names in at least two ways. First consider the following dialogues:

Dialogue 1

Child (C) : Look! (pointing at teddy)
Mother (M) : Yes, that's teddy.
       C   : Look! (still pointing at teddy)

Dialogue 2

C : Dat? (pointing at teddy)
M : What's that? That's teddy.
C : Dat? (pointing at toy car).

Dialogue 3

C : Whatdat? (pointing at teddy).
M : That's teddy.
C : Teddy. Teddy.
M : Yes, that's right. That's teddy.

The three dialogues are representative of a brief exchange between a mother and her child at three different stages in the child's development, around 15 months, 18 months and 21 months.

Dialogue 1 suggests that the child has not yet conceived of the possibility that objects, in this case teddy, can have names. Of course, it may be that the child can name objects but chooses not to do so on this occasion. We would need to consider a large enough sample of the child's own utterances at, say 15 months, to rule out this possibility. In fact, when we actually consider some real data for 15 month olds we find that dialogue 1 is fairly representative of many of the mother–child exchanges and that the child does not seem to attempt to name objects. Notice that in dialogue 1 both the phonetic and object concept conditions for the act of naming would seem to be fulfilled. The child is capable of producing adult-like words ("Look!") and would seem to have a fairly shrewd conception that the teddy is an object which can be pointed at i.e. it has a distinctive and reliable existence. Despite the fulfilment of the phonetic and object concept conditions, the act of naming does not seem to have been mastered. The connecting link has not yet been established.

Dialogue 2 presents the child language researcher with a difficult problem of interpretation. Many parents will recognise the questioning utterance "Dat?" as one of the early utterances of their child. They will also probably remember the overwhelming tendency to interpret the child's utterance as a shortened form of the adult utterance "What's that?" Indeed, the hypothetical mother in dialogue 2 responds to the child by explicitly interpreting the child's utterance before going on to name the object for the child. If the mother's interpretation of the child is correct, then such behaviour by the child would seem to be a good indicator that he has mastered the act of naming. And if the child is asking for the object's name, then he has a clear expectation that objects have names and he can use words to name them. In short, if the child uses the utterance "Dat?" in an appropriate context (e.g. whilst pointing at an object in the presence of a listener whom the child has reason to believe can supply a name) and the "What's that?" interpretation is correct, then we have good reason to believe that the child has mastered the act of naming.

However, we must consider the evidence for interpreting the child's utterance as a request that an object be named. Just because the utterance sounds like "What's that?" is insufficient grounds for claiming that it has an identical meaning to the adult form. Of course, in the final analysis it is impossible to be sure what the child means by what he says. However, we can try to rule out various possible interpretations by considering how the child uses such utterances in different situations. For example, if the child used the utterance "Dat?" whilst pointing at an object but whilst no one was present, we might feel less inclined to believe that the child was asking for a name even when he used it in the presence of others. Alternatively, if the child also used the same expression whilst reaching to grab an object, whether in the presence of another person or not, we might feel more inclined to interpret the utterance as some kind of generalised comment that accompanies his gestural interactions with objects. Of course, just because the child might use the same expression in different situations does not preclude the possibility that it is being used for different purposes on each occasion e.g. asking for a name and for requesting to be given an object. Adult language is full of expressions which can fulfil more than one purpose. "It's cold in here", may simply be a statement of fact or a request for someone to switch on the radiator or close the window. Our interpretation of a single expression depends on the context of use. Why shouldn't we attribute the same multi-functional character to children's utterances?

I think, as a general rule, we should be prepared to give children the benefit of the doubt in our interpretations of their utterances, unless we have good reason to question the hypothesised underlying meaning. In dialogue 2, there is reasonable doubt that the child is asking for the name of the object. When the mother names the object for the child ("That's teddy".), the child makes no acknowledgement that he has registered and understood his mother's utterance. Instead, the child simply points at another object and re-peats the original expression. One might reasonably expect that if the child was asking for the object's name, he would make some attempt to verbalise the label that his mother provided. Instead, his behaviour seems more directed at playing a social game with his mother whereby he maintains a satisfying interaction through the medium of gesture and voice. This game would appear to have simi-lar characteristics to the interaction described in dialogue 1, except that the child now shifts objects on consecutive contributions.

Again, our conclusion that the child's "Dat?" does not indicate an understanding of naming must be tentative. Just because the child does not proceed to name the object explicitly in response to the mother's contribution, does not rule out the possibility that he is remembering the name for use at a later time. We might evaluate this possibility by collecting further data on the child's language to hear if he subsequently uses the name his mother provided. If the child does not subsequently produce the name and at a later point in his development seems to have to learn the name from scratch, then we would seem further justified in our conclusion that the child was not requesting the name of the object. Furthermore, if the child does not appear to be using words to name other objects at the time of dialogue 2, we would have greater reason to believe that he had not yet mastered the act of naming.

It should be clear by now that **any** interpretation of a child's language must be based on a broad range of knowledge of the beha-viour of that child. Very often, this knowledge is not available to the child language researcher and we must rely on the information and intuitions that parents can provide. However, in the long run,

42

we must try to collect intensive longitudinal data for individual children for it is only in this way that we can carefully evaluate the child's developing linguistic skills. To date, the data, though inconclusive, suggest that children who engage in interactions like dialogue 2 have not yet mastered the act of naming. They use expressions like "Dat?" in a variety of situations, often in the absence of another person. They fail to respond to the mother's labeling and do not seem to name other objects. Finally, they seem to need to learn the names from scratch at a later date.

In contrast, the child of **dialogue 3** does respond to his mother's labelling in a way that suggests that he really does desire to know the name of the object. Of course, we cannot conclude on the basis of dialogue 3 alone that the child is naming, any more than dialogue 2 proves that the child is unable to name. It is quite conceivable that the child of dialogue 3 is merely **imitating** his mother's utterance. It is not necessary to attribute to the child the conception that "Teddy" is the name of the object pointed at. However, if we continue to observe the child's language and notice him use the word "Teddy" whilst pointing at Teddy on subsequent occasions, or perhaps even use "Teddy" to talk about other teddies, then we would seem to have greater reason to trust in our interpretation that the child has named the object.

You might have got the feeling that my analysis of dialogues 1 to 3 has been rather like trying to suck blood from a stone. The conversational interactions provide scant evidence for what the child does or does not know. However, it is important to remember that I have set each of these dialogues in the context of our, supposed, knowledge of other aspects of the child's behaviour. Without this extra knowledge it would be impossible to come to a final conclusion on the problem of naming.

Before leaving dialogues 1 to 3 I should like to extract an extra drop of blood from the stone. There are several interesting developments over the course of the 3 interactions which may have important implications for how the child **learns** to name. First, it is clear in dialogue 1 that the child is engaging in a process of **joint attention** with the mother. Both partners in the conversation are able to focus simultaneously on the same object and so establish a channel of communication. The capacity of the child to participate in a process of joint attention with the mother is clearly important, if the child is to learn the name of objects. By the time the child is interacting with his mother in conversations like dialogue 2, he has already developed his skills of joint attention. He now shifts quickly from one object to another whilst maintaining a satisfying social interaction. In so doing, the child may well be contrasting one object with another and consequently giving his mother the opportunity to provide him with a variety of names to distinguish the objects. Even though the child may not be able to conceptualise the mother's linguistic behaviour as an act of naming, the contrastive process must be an important factor in the child discovering that different objects have different names.

Finally, the act of imitation may be more important in learning how to name, than I have given it credit for. By imitating his parents, the child may be acquiring a vocabulary of terms that are useful to him when he eventually discovers that objects have names. Furthermore, the tendency to imitate may play an important role in learning that objects have names. The child's active imitation of the parent on a number of different occasions, perhaps with the same object, may lead to an **insight** on behalf of the child; an insight arising out of repeated experiences of imitating a particular sound in the presence of a particular object. Of course, imitation does not explain how this insight, i.e. that objects have names, comes about. But the child's tendency for imitation may play an important role in the setting up of suitable conditions for the discovery of this insight.

I suggested earlier that there are at least 2 ways in which we might recognise that young children have developed the expectation that objects have names. We have just considered the first possibility, namely recognising the child's ability to ask for the name of an object. The second possibility is related to the child's vocabulary growth. If we attempt to count the number of new words that a child masters during different periods of development, we find that the rate of increase of his vocabulary is not regular. That is, he learns more new words in some periods of development than in others. Of particular interest in this connection, is the sudden increase in rate of vocabulary development that occurs for many children during the latter half of the second year. Figure 3.2. exemplifies how dramatic this increase often is.

Vocabulary Scores for Jens

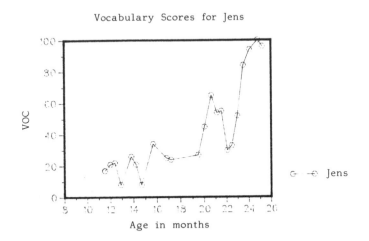

G——⊙ Jens

Source: Plunkett, 1985.

Fig. 3.2.

Typically, children have a slow but gradual increase in vocabulary during the first half of their second year, but then comes what amounts to an explosion in their vocabulary. A number of researchers, notably McShane (1979), attribute this vocabulary explosion to the child's discovery that objects and actions can be named. In other words, McShane takes the position that during the earliest stages of language development, words are not used to name objects but would seem to have an instrumental function e.g. the child uses words to achieve a particular goal like being given something or attracting someone's attention. Single-word utterances like "More" or "Hallo" or "Look" are often used precisely for these purposes. The child's mastery of such words increases with age, both in his capacity to use them effectively and in the range of expressions at his disposal, but this increase is but a gradual one in comparison to the rate of development that shortly follows. McShane points out that

45

when the vocabulary explosions occurs, the increases are not due to the child's sudden mastery of more function (instrumental) words. Rather, the increases are almost entirely due to the child learning names for objects. That the new words are names is evidenced by the child's way of using the words e.g. using a word to refer to a variety of objects that come from the same class (Teddy) and his emergent capacity to ask for names and use the information he is given in response. Since the child has not previously used language to name objects, this dramatic emergence of naming vocabulary strongly suggests a sudden discovery by the child that objects have names.

In summary, there are two ways in which we may recognise that children have the expectation that objects have names. First, there is the qualitative evidence which relates to the way in which children **use** early words. Secondly, there is the evidence as to the nature of the quantitative changes in the child's early vocabulary growth. Both pieces of evidence, qualitative and quantitative, point to the conclusion that young children do **not** use language to name objects at the very beginning of language development. Such language would seem to have a more instrumental character. The act of naming would seem to be a skill that the child discovers rather suddenly later in his second year. The question then arises as to how the child makes this discovery.

3.4   Explanations of Naming

Earlier in this chapter, I considered some of the basic conditions that need to be fulfilled before a child can master the act of naming. First, it was observed that the child must be able to produce a sign, be it a word or a hand gesture, with which to perform the act of naming. Secondly, it was reasoned that the child should be able to conceptualise the world as consisting of objects which are distinct from one another. Without this conceptualisation, it would not be possible to use names to distinguish objects in the world simply because there would be no objects to distinguish. In this respect, it was argued that achievement of full object permanence was not a necessary condition for the ability to distinguish objects from one another. Developments at least as early as stage 4 of object per-

manence indicate that the child has mastered the ability to differentiate objects. Therefore, from the point of view of the object and
the sign, the conditions for naming are fulfilled by the time the
child produces his very first utterances. Explanations as to why the
child is delayed in his mastery of the act of naming must look to
other sources.

The core of the problem seems to focus on how the child conceptualises the **link** between the **sign** and the **object** as a naming
link. As we have already seen, the earliest links between signs and
objects would seem to be instrumental in character. The naming link
is a qualitatively different conceptualisation. How can we explain
the manner in which the child comes to achieve this understanding?
McShane (1979) offers the explanation that the child's discovery of
naming is based on "insight". This insight is a sudden affair and
thus accounts for the dramatic increase in the child's vocabulary of
names. McShane argues that the insight is based upon the child's
experience of ritual naming games played together with his parents.
Dialogues 1 and 2, described earlier in this chapter, might consti-
tute examples of such ritual naming games where the child partici-
pates in a process of joint attention with the mother. During the
course of these games, the child comes to associate particular words
with particular objects, even though he does not yet conceptualise
the word as the **name** of the object:

> I would suggest that the child does not possess the con-
> cept of naming when he or she first learns to pair words
> with objects in rituals such as story-book reading. My
> further suggestion is that the words the child initially
> learns in these situations are learnt as a means of parti-
> cipating in a ritual activity that concerns talking about
> objects. The child first learns the words and later learns
> that these words are names. The key element in learning
> that words are names is an insight by the child that **the
> behaviour previously engaged in** in ritual situations (such
> as picture-book reading) can be taken to constitute a spe-
> cial type of language-use: naming. (McShane, 1979, p.
> 890).

McShane's account of the development of naming conforms well
with the data described in his own longitudinal study of 6 children's language development, as well as that of studies conducted by
Nelson (1973) and Halliday (1975). Furthermore, there is a strong

precedent in the psychological literature for appealing to "insight" as an important factor in the process of learning (e.g. Kohler, 1925). However, appeals to insight often leave the researcher wondering just how the insight comes about. Reformulations of insight such as "a relatively sudden realisation of some previously unseen structural relationship", do little to satiate the researcher's desire to achieve better understanding of the process. If we could better understand how the child achieves his insight then our understanding of how the child learns how to name will be much deeper.

One possible explanation of how the child comes to learn the act of naming relates to the child's developing **symbolic** skills. You will recall from chapter two our discussion of Piaget's theory that children have to learn the capacity for symbolic representation during the course of the sensorimotor period. The symbolic capacity, when it is fully flowered, enables the child to represent objects to himself in the form of some kind of mental image, even when they are absent. The child's mastery of object permanence is a manifestation of the underlying skill of symbolic representation. It seems reasonable to suggest that just as the symbolic capacity may be important for the attainment of full object permanence, so may the symbolic capacity be important for the discovering of the act of naming. After all, a name plays the role of a symbol that stands for, or substitutes the object itself. Thus when we use the word "dog" as a name, it is a symbol for the object. The kind of link which connects a symbol (be it an image or an abstract character) to its referent would appear to be the same kind of link which connects a word to an object in the act of naming. Thus, the development of a symbolic capacity is an important condition for the child's discovery of naming. Corrigan (1978) makes a similar point in her own study:

> The study also found a general correspondence between the attainment of the final rank of the object permanence scale (Rank 21) and an increase in the child's total vocabulary. Presumably, language growth at this time would not be due to object permanence development per se, but to the increased symbolic capacity necessary to perform on both tasks. (Corrigan, 1978, p. 187).

Unfortunately, what is missing from Corrigan's account is an explicit concern with the act of naming. Nevertheless, she does report that the greatest increases in total vocabulary did not occur until or after the time each child had reached full object permanence. When we interpret this finding in the light of McShane's claim that the vocabulary explosion in the latter half of the child's second year reflects a discovery of the act of naming, it is not a great step to infer that the act of naming must also await the development of the same symbolic capacity that underlies full object permanence. In McShane's study, dramatic vocabulary increases are said to reflect the mastery of naming. In Corrigan's study, dramatic vocabulary increases are said to reflect the attainment of full object permanence. The connection between naming and full object permanence would seem obvious.

However, in a later article, McShane & Whittaker (1982) have argued that the development of a mature symbolic capacity as indicated by the achievement of full object permanence is an unnecessarily complex capacity for the mastery of the symbolic relation of naming between a word and an object. They point out, that naming does not necessarily involve the ability to refer to an object in its absence. The act of naming can occur in the presence of objects, provided the child conceives the relation between the word and the present object as a symbolic one.

> According to Piaget (1945) a child can be said to use language symbolically when he uses words to recall absent objects. Uttering a word in the absence of a referent is not in itself sufficient; there must be evidence that the word is uttered in the service of recalling some event. It is readily apparent why Piaget uses the criterion of verbal recall. If a child uses a word to refer to an object in the absence of that object then the word is obviously intended to represent the object and can unequivocally be said to be a symbol for the object. The criterion is certainly adequate for inferring the presence of a symbolic relation between word and object. But it is adequate only at the cost of being a conservative criterion. Theoretically, there is no reason why reference in the presence of an object cannot be symbolic (so long as an adequate criterion for inferring a symbolic capacity can be established). Using the criterion of recall automatically rules out consideration of such cases. (McShane & Whittaker, 1982, p. 6-7)

Preliminary Approaches to Language Development

Of course, the whole problem for this attempt to undermine the primacy of a mature symbolic capacity for naming, hinges upon one's analysis of the relationship between words and objects before a mature symbolic capacity is achieved. Can an entity (e.g. a word) be said to have a symbolic relation to an object, if the entity cannot be used to recall that object in its absence? McShane & Whittaker argue that it can. Presumably, they mean that an object has the power to "conjure up" the relevant symbol (word) for that object before the child is able to "conjure up" the symbol for himself in the absence of the object. In either case, the symbolic relation between word and object is the same. Self-generation of symbols is just a more highly developed capacity than object-stimulated symbols.

Before we become too absorbed in philosophical issues, it is worth considering some empirical evidence that does indeed support McShane & Whittaker's claim that naming occurs prior to the development of a mature symbolic capacity. In her study of the relationship between language development and object permanence, Corrigan distinguished between two classes of words which she called function terms and substantive forms respectively. Roughly, this distinction corresponds to the one we have drawn in this chapter between instrumental words and words used to name. Corrigan was interested in testing Bloom's (1973) earlier claim that function forms were the dominant words in the child's vocabulary prior to achievement of sensorimotor stage 6 and that substantive forms were not reliably used until after this stage. Corrigan found no such evidence. Substantives were used just as frequently (albeit at a low frequency) as function forms before the achievement of level 21 of object permanence. In other words, children had begun to name objects before they had developed a mature symbolic capacity as defined by Piaget.

At first glance, these results may seem somewhat contradictory. Corrigan reports that children are naming before the achievement of level 21 of object permanence but that vocabulary development does not really "take off" until after level 21. On the other hand, McShane argues for the vocabulary explosion as evidence of the mastery of the act of naming. However, a closer look at Corrigan's vocabulary data leads one to suspect the role of level 21 in the vocabulary explosion. For all three of Corrigan's subjects, substantial ground in vocabulary development had been made prior to the achievement of level 21. For example, two subjects had achieved already by level 19 vocabulary spans that were at least 50% of their vocabulary span at level 21 whilst the third subject had achieved 25% of his level 21 vocabulary span by level 19. These figures do not suggest that a dramatic increase in vocabulary occurred around level 21 of object permanence. At least, not the kind of dramatic increases suggested by fig. 3.2. If we are to conclude the primacy of any particular level of object permanence from Corrigan's data then it must be level 15 (the onset of stage 6 of the sensorimotor period). Corrigan's data show that before this stage, vocabulary development is more or less dormant. However, once level 15 is attained the vocabularies begin to expand - perhaps not explosively but nevertheless at a significantly changed rate of development.

It is instructive to consider the different criteria that are necessary for demonstrating a competence at levels 15 and 21 of object permanence respectively. At level 15, the child must be able to find an object after it has been hidden (without the child being able to see the hiding) under a screen A and then invisibly displaced in the hand to a second screen B. Typically the child will search under A and then look under B. At level 21, the object is invisibly hidden under screen A again but left in position whilst the hand "pretends" to invisibly hide the object under two more screens B and C, consecutively. The child must first search under screen C, then B, and finally A before finding the object.

From an adult perspective, the test at level 21 would seem more to resemble the magician's trick-playing than having to do with establishing that the child has mastered the symbolic capacity. However, the child's behaviour on the test at level 21 clearly demonstrates that he is aware that objects do not need to move even though he might have expected a hand to be moving it. The child needs to establish the independent existence of the object from the actions of both himself and others. Indeed, the magician's ability to entertain audiences with such tricks probably derives from a tendency to relapse into a less sophisticated level of object permanence in situations with which we are unfamiliar; a tendency which Piaget calls "Decalage" and can be observed over a wide variety of skills both in children and adults. Success on level 21 demonstrates the child's capacity to manipulate a symbolic representation of the object and imagine it in different places. At level 15 the child is **not** required to abstract the independent existence of the object from the actions of others. Indeed, he is explicitly expected to use his memory of the movement of the experimenter's hand to find the object after he has failed to find it under screen A. However, the child is required to be able to conceive of objects when he cannot see them and imagine their shifting from one place to another through the action of another person. This ability to conceive of an object in its absence and imagine displacements of an image of that object shows that the child has already achieved a substantial understanding of the symbol. Furthermore, this level of symbolic skill may well be adequate for the discovery of the act of naming.

McShane and Whittaker would thus appear to be justified in claiming that a fully matured symbolic capacity is an unnecessarily complex prerequisite for the achievement of naming. However, the claim, as I have developed it, rests upon the assumption that the degree of symbolic skill achieved by level 15 of object permanence is, indeed, sufficient for the symbolic relation of naming between word and object. In his theory of naming, McShane (1979) suggests that the child initially learns a number of object-word mappings as part of a ritual naming game before he learns that the words act as names for the objects. These object-word mappings are not the same as the symbolic, naming relation between word and object. Otherwise, the child would have mastered already the act of naming. The discovery of the symbolic relation between word and object is, indeed, the discovery of the act of naming. However, we must ask what it is that the child learns when he learns the symbolic relation between word and object. It must be more than a "conjuring up" of a symbol by an object, for that is no more than saying there is an object-word mapping. What is lacking from McShane's account is an explanation of how words become symbols for the child.

It is, of course, unfair to single out McShane for failing to provide such an account. Piaget, although he **describes** the child's symbolic capacities and various other developments, does not explain **how** the child comes to conceive of the symbolic relation between a word and an object, any more than does McShane when he points to sudden increases in vocabulary as an index of the symbolic capacity. It is difficult to criticise McShane for appealing to the ill-understood process of insight as an explanation of the development of naming, when we find it so difficult to expain how the child develops the symbolic skill itself. Indeed, one can only concur with McShane's lament that

> " ... a more detailed investigation of the development of symbolic behaviour, including naming, will be needed to be carried out before the precise role of a symbolic function in development is determined." (McShane, 1979, p. 895).

3.5 Concluding Remarks

In this chapter we have been concerned with how the child learns the act of naming. Although we have pointed to a number of skills which the child must master in order to discover that things have names, we have been unable to give a satisfactory account of how he goes about acquiring these skills. In a book about language development, an account of the act of naming deserves a special place. On the surface, naming would seem to be a distinctly linguistic skill. But we have seen how explanations of the development of naming tend to make use of concepts that are not exclusively linguistic.

The concept of the symbol has a special status in our study. The human use of language is a symbolic skill par excellence. Furthermore, human thought processes which involve the representation and manipulation of knowledge clearly use the symbol as the basis of these mental acts. It is, therefore, not at all surprising that the concept of the symbol has been considered central in most modern accounts of language and thought. Indeed, it is probably in the general symbolic nature of human activity that the key to our understanding of the relationship between language and thought lies. However, drawing connections between the symbolic aspects of language and thought is not enough. We must also discover how the symbolic skill is realised in each of these areas of human activity individually. Identifying, the acquisition of object permanence and pointing to the symbolic nature of this skill is by no means an explanation of how the symbol comes to be used in human thought processes. And it is certainly not an explanation of the symbolic nature of language. Even if we did understand how the child developed his symbolic capacities to achieve object permanence, we would still be left with the task of explaining how the child realises his symbolic capacity in language.

On the other side of the coin, it is reasonable to hope that an understanding of the emergence of symbolic skills in one domain will contribute to an understanding of that emergence in other domains. Only time and progress will tell. Naming and object permanence both rely on the symbolic skill. That much is clear. The nature of the similarities and differences of this reliance in the two domains remains to be discovered.

4   THE LINGUISTIC LEGACY

4.1   Phrase Structure Grammar

The protagonists of the chapter two, Whorf, Piaget and Vygotsky all believed that language and thought had important connections with each other. Their views varied as to the nature of the connection. But that there was some kind of connection, all were agreed. In this chapter, we shall consider the views of a living authority who does not believe the language and thought are inextricably intertwined. That person is the American linguist, Noam Chomsky. To understand the nature of Chomsky's (1957) position we need to take a brief look at his theory of **Transformational Grammar.** It is a theory of structural linguistics, formulated in the late fifties when fundamental changes were also taking place in psychological science. In fact, unlike his predecessors who considered linguistics a branch of the science of anthropology, Chomsky felt that linguistics is more properly placed in the realm of psychology.

In general, linguists attempt to study the grammars of different languages. This means that they try to write structural descriptions of parts of a language, say sentences, in order to discover the rules to which those parts of the language conform. For example, a fragment of English grammar might look like the following:

Rule 1: Sentence	(S) ⟶ Noun Phrase(NP)+Verb Phrase(VP)
Rule 2: Noun Phrase	(NP) ⟶ Article (Art.) + Noun (N)
Rule 3: Verb Phrase	(VP) ⟶ Verb (V) + Noun Phrase (NP)
lexi- ⎫ cal ⎬ rules ⎭	Art. ⟶ A, the Verb ⟶ throws, hits, gives Noun ⟶ boy, girl, ball

Table 4.1.

This grammar is interpreted such that for each rule, the symbol on the left-hand side of the arrow can be replaced by the symbol or symbols to the right of the arrow. We could represent these rules in another way by using branching hierarchical structures or tree diagrams as in Figure 4.1. Try checking these **tree diagrams** against Rules 1-3 above.

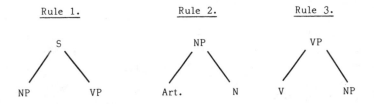

Fig. 4.1.

However, what does all this mean? How do these rules provide us with a simple grammar of English? The linguist's system begins to look clearer if we try to put these rules together. For example, you will notice that the lower ends of the branch (or "nodes" as they are usually called) of rule 1, i.e. NP and VP, are also the starting nodes for rules 2 and 3. We can put these rules together to form a more complicated hierarchical structure or tree as in figure 4.2.

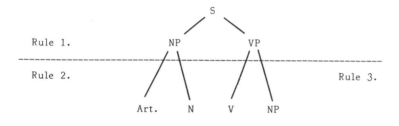

Rule 1.

Rule 2.   Rule 3.

Fig. 4.2.

Again, try checking how I constructed this structure by comparing it to the trees described in figure 4.1. In fact, I started with rule 1 and then applied rules 2 and 3 to the NP and VP nodes respectively. If we now look at the bottom row of symbols of the tree diagram in figure 4.2. we notice that one of the nodes (NP) can still be expanded according to rule 2. Applying rule 2 to this node yields the tree diagram in figure 4.3.

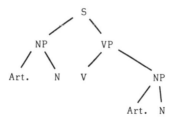

Fig. 4.3.

It is probably becoming a bit clearer how the rules provide us with a simple grammar of English sentences. Now look at the bottom-most node of each branch in the tree diagram. You will notice that there are no rules for expanding these symbols in terms of other symbols. However, there are a set of **lexical rules** for replacing these symbols with other symbols, namely words. If we now apply these lexical rules to the bottom-most elements in the tree diagram of figure 4.3., we obtain figure 4.4.

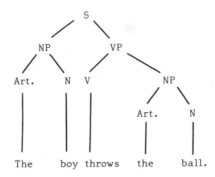

Fig. 4.4.

The bottom-most elements in figure 4.4. happen to be words. There are no rules present in the grammar which tell us how to replace or rewrite these elements in terms of other elements. They are, therefore, the **terminal elements** in the structure.

In the above process, we have constructed a structual description of the English sentence, "The boy throws the ball". Linguists call the type of grammar described by the rules in Table 4.1., a **Phrase Structure Grammar**. There are a number of interesting things that we can learn from phrase structure grammars. First, they enable us to assign the words of a language to grammatical categories like nouns, verbs, and articles. In the present case, these three grammatical categories provide an exhaustive coverage of the phrase structure grammar's basic grammatical elements. A more complicated grammar would include many more like adjective, pronoun, adverb, preposition, etc. Nevertheless, in each case the grammar provides a grammatical classification of the words in a language. This classification is helpful because it enables us to describe the role that a word plays in the sentence structure. For example, we know from our grammar (see Table 4.1.), that if a word is classified as a verb then its role in the sentence structure is unambiguously assigned as in figure 4.4. That is, the verb is part of the verb phrase of the sentence. However, the grammatical category noun does not unambiguously assign words a role in the sentence. The noun is a constituent component of the higher order grammatical category, noun phrase. The structural description given in figure 4.4. shows that the noun phrase occurs in two different roles in the structure; either as a direct constituent of the sentence (S) node or as a constituent of the verb phrase (VP) node. We know the precise structural role of a noun in a sentence only if we know the noun phrase to which it belongs.

This type of information may seem a rather abstract and even arbitrary classification of the words in a language. However, the classification of words into grammatical categories like noun, verb and article, together with the assignment of these grammatical categories themselves into other categories like noun phrase and verb phrase provides us with an insight into the word-order rules of a language. Our ability to understand sentences like, "The girl hits the boy", relies on our knowledge of word-order rules of English. For example, we know that it is the girl who is doing the hitting and the boy who is being hit. This knowledge is reflected in the phrase structure description given to the sentence "The girl hits the boy" which is identical to the structure in figure 4.4. (You might like to try following through the rules again to see how the sentence is generated by the grammar). For example, the phrase "the girl", is assigned to a different noun phrase than "the boy" and these two noun phrases each occur in different contexts in the structural description of the sentence. These differences in the structural positions of the noun phrases in the sentence are the key to our knowledge of the word order rules. The noun phrase which is directly dominated by the sentence (S) node is the subject of the action described in the sentence. The noun phrase which is dominated by the verb phrase (VP) node is the object of the action described in the sentence. Since "the girl" belongs to a noun phrase of the first type we know that it must be the subject of the sentence. That is, the first noun phrase in the sentence, as defined by the phrase structure description is the subject of the sentence. Similarly, the second noun phrase in the structure indicates the object of the sentence. In other words, the categories described by the grammar together with their position in their structure of the sentence help us interpret the word-order rules of the language.

It is worth noting that not all languages order their words in the same way as English, i.e. subject - verb - object. For example, some languages, like Japanese, set the object before the verb i.e. subject - object - verb. This gives rise to sentences which we may paraphrase in the following way; "The girl the boy hits". It is reasonable to suppose that a native speaker of English, on hearing such a sentence, would be uncertain as to who was doing the hitting, the girl or the boy. However, if we showed him the phrase structure description of this sentence and explained the significance of the structure then he would be able to decipher its meaning. Figure 4.5. provides just such a description:

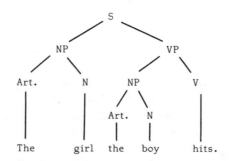

Fig. 4.5.

Here, the noun phrase directly dominated by the sentence (S) node is still the subject of the sentence whilst the noun phrase dominated by the verb phrase (VP) node is still the object of the sentence. We have not changed the internal structural relations of the components of the structure. All we have changed is the way the structure orders the words, or terminal elements, of the structure. This can be done simply by changing rule 3 in table 4.1. so that it reads:

Rule 3a: Verb Phrase (VP) ⟶ Noun Phrase (NP) + Verb (V)

Thus, phrase structure grammars help us to assign the words of a sentence to a particular structural description. We can then use our knowledge of the structural description to discover the relationship of the words in the sentence to each other.

We can now begin to see why Chomsky believes that linguistics is a branch of psychology rather than anthropology. If grammars, like the one we have discussed above, help linguists to understand and interpret the regularities underlying the sentences of a language, then it is feasible that ordinary native speakers may unconsciously make use of this knowledge when understanding and producing sentences. They too may make use of the knowledge that sentences can be analysed in terms of noun phrases and verb phrases, and use the structural relations between these constituents to construct and understand sentences. Clearly, the native speaker is not consciously aware of these linguistic rules and structures. But that does not mean that he does not know them. To return to a distinction that I introduced in chapter two, it is possible to "know how" to perform some skill without "knowing that" the skill incorporates a particular set of structural components. In this case, the native speaker "knows how" to produce and understand grammatically correct sentences of English even though he does not "know that" he is able to do this by virtue of his knowledge of the rules of English. He can function perfectly well without "knowing that" he possesses this knowledge. Chomsky calls this underlying linguistic knowledge, the native speaker's **linguistic competence**. It is the linguist's job to make this competence explicit.

In making the native speaker's linguistic competence explicit, the linguist may be helping the psychologist understand how people are able to use language as easily as they do. After all, language is just as much an example of human behaviour as any other activity we might perform. Indeed, some would argue that our language skills are the most human of our diverse range of activities. If linguistics provides us with an understanding of how people are able to use language then it is clearly contributing to a theory of psychology. Chomsky argues that the primary goal of linguistics is to describe the native speaker's linguistic competence. That is, linguistics should have an explanatory function in addition to its descriptive function. Linguistics is descriptively adequate in so far as it is successful in ascribing structural descriptions to all the sentences of the language. Linguistics is explanatorily adequate in so far as these descriptions fit the native speaker's own linguistic competence. It is Chomsky's demand for the explanatory adequacy of linguistic theories that sets linguistics in the realm of psychology.

What evidence is there, then, that people make use of the kind of knowledge that linguists call phrase structure grammars? Or to put the question in a slightly more formal way, are phrase structure grammars an explanatorily adequate description of the native speaker's linguistic competence? An experimental study of native speaker's abilities to remember lists of sentences sheds some light on this question. Johnson (1965) asked subjects to remember long lists of sentences so that they could recall them at a later time. Most of the sentences were short and simple like;

4.1.) The tall boy saved the dying woman.

4.2.) The house across the street is burning.

The subjects were then asked to recall these sentences. Johnson recorded their responses so that he could analyse them in detail at a later date. Johnson was particularly interested in investigating the errors that the subjects made. He analysed the errors by calculating for each word recalled, the probability that the word is incorrectly recalled given that the preceding word is correctly recalled. For example, in sentence 4.1.) above, Johnson measured the probability that the word "saved" would be recalled given that the subject had correctly recalled the word "boy". This measure is called the **Transition Error Probability** (TEP). It is a probability measure because it gives us an idea of how often a word was correctly recalled. Clearly, for one subject the probability is 1 or 0, i.e. right or wrong. However, for a large number of subjects an average in between these extremes will be obtained. Figure 4.6. gives a summary of the results that Johnson obtained for sentence 4.1.).

Consider first the transition error probabilities (TEPs) as summarised in the histogram below the tree diagram. The height of each bar gives a measure of the likelihood that an error was made in remembering a word given that the previous word was remembered correctly. The first thing to notice is that the TEPs are not all the same. For example, subjects were much more likely to forget the word "saved" than the word "woman" given that they had correctly recalled the preceding word. One possible explanation of this phenomenon is that the strength of the associations between consecutive words in the sentence differ. Thus, "woman" is more strongly associated with "dying" than "saved" is with "boy". However, such an explanation begs the question as to how these associations are formed. Furthermore, Johnson found that the TEPs between two identical words varied from sentence to sentence. For example, the TEP between "boy" and "saved" was much lower in another sentence.

Johnson suggested that the varying TEP could best be understood in terms of the phrase structures of the sentences. Consider the phrase structure of sentence 4.1.) as described in the tree diagram of figure 4.6. This tree was derived in precisely the same way as the structure in figure 4.4. except that Rule 2 from table 4.1. has

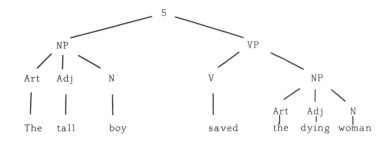

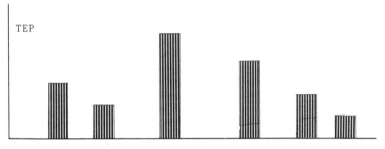

Fig. 4.6.

now been modified to allow for the possibility of including an
adjective in the noun phrase. You will notice that the largest errors
occur between words where there is a major break in the phrase
structure of the sentence. In sentence 4.1.) the greatest number of
errors are between "boy" and "saved" and between "saved" and
"the". These correspond to positions in the phrase structure where
the S node decomposes into the NP and VP branches and VP node
splits into the V and NP branches. These are the highest level
branchings in the structure. This suggests that subjects learn sentences in phrase groups as defined by the grammar; when part of a
phrase is learned, the rest of it tends to be learned as well. Figure
4.7. summarises Johnson's results for sentence 4.2.). The phrase
structure is more complicated as a result of the introduction of rules
for prepositional phrases (PP) and auxiliary verbs (aux.). However,
the pattern of errors still correlates with the phrase structure of the
sentence with the most errors occurring at major breaks in the structure.

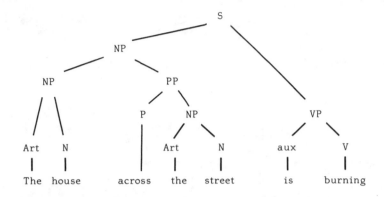

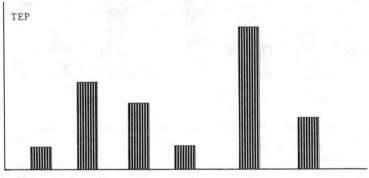

Fig. 4.7.

Johnson's experiment demonstrates that the structure of a sentence, as defined by the grammar, can influence an individual's behaviour in an observable way. This suggests that the individual is, in some sense, in possession of knowledge corresponding to a phrase structure grammar. Otherwise, why does he behave (or rather forget!) in the way he does. Phrase structure grammar, as described by linguists, would appear to have some psychological reality.

That the phrase structure of a sentence has some psychological reality, i.e. it is representative of knowledge possessed by the native speaker, has also been demonstrated in a different type of experiment by Garrett, Bever and Fodor (1966). Their study investigated a subject's ability to judge the timing of a short burst of noise, which sounded like a click, in relation to the words in a sentence. A sentence was played to the subject on a tape recorder. At some instant during the recording a click was sounded. The subject had to report where the click occurred in the sentence. An example of two of the sentences used by Garrett et al. is given below:

4.3.) As a direct result of their new invention's influence **the company** was given an award.

4.4.) The retiring chairman whose methods still greatly influence **the company** was given an award.

The sentences were constructed from spliced tapes so that there could be no auditory differences between the target words in each sentence, i.e. "the company", that might influence the subject's behaviour. When each sentence was played to the subject, the click occurred objectively at the centre of the phrase "the company". However, with sentence 4.3.), subjects reported that they heard the click between the words "influence" and "the". On the other hand, in sentence 4.4.) subjects reported that the click occurred between the words "company" and "was". That is, the judgement of click position in the two sentences is not only wrong but in opposite directions in each sentence. Garrett et al. point out that in each case the click has been displaced towards a major break in the phrase structure of each sentence. They argue that this has occurred as a consequence of the psychological principle that collection of elements which form a coherent group, resist interruption by irrelevant stimuli. Hence the irrelevant stimulus, the click, is displaced by the psychologically perceived group, in this case, the phrase. The strength of this effect is demonstrated by the opposite displacements in the two sentences. In sentence 4.3.), the click is subjectively displaced backward in time to the beginning of a phrase constituent of the sentence. In sentence 4.4.) the click is subjectively displaced forward in time to the end of a major phrase constituent. If Garrett et al.'s explanation of the click displacement effect is correct, then their results also support the notion that phrase constituents, as defined by the grammar, have a psychological reality for the listener. Somehow or other the listener is sensitive to the phrase structure of the sentence even though he may not be able to explicitly describe it to us.

Preliminary Approaches to Language Development

4.2. Transformational Grammar

Experiments like Johnson's and Garrett et al.'s provide persuasive evidence that the linguist's structural descriptions can tell us something about how people use language. However, their results do not prove that phrase structure grammars are the best way to describe the linguistic competence possessed by the native speaker. Chomsky has argued that there are a number of psychological aspects of a native speaker's linguistic competence which cannot be explained in terms of phrase structure grammars. Consider the following set of sentences.

> 4.5.) Stephen is eating the cake.
> 4.6.) Stephen is not eating the cake.
> 4.7.) The cake is being eaten by Stephen.
> 4.8.) Is Stephen eating the cake?

A phrase structure grammar would assign a different structural description to each of these sentences. Yet we know that all four sentences are in some way related. For example, if pressed we could think of some more sentences that are similarly related;

> 4.9.) Is the cake being eaten by Stephen?

Chomsky argues that a grammar which attempts to assign structural descriptions to the sentences of a language, should also be able to explain the source of the native speaker's intuitions that sentences, like those above, are somehow related. Phrase structure grammars are clearly inadequate for this purpose.

Another reason for deeming phrase structure grammars inadequate for the purpose of capturing native speakers intuitions, relates to the way they deal with ambiguous sentences. Consider the sentence:

> 4.10.) They are visiting relatives.

Native speakers of English will quickly discover that this sentence has two meanings, i.e. it is ambiguous. The ambiguity centres on the role of the word "visiting" in the sentence. In one meaning, it plays the role of adjective. In the other meaning, it is a present participle in the verb. A phrase structure grammar is able to capture this ambiguity by assigning the sentence two alternative structural descriptions as in figure 4.8.

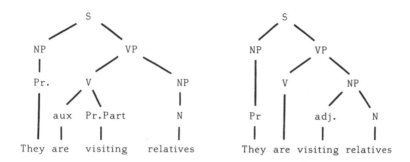

Fig. 4.8.

However, now consider the following ambiguous sentence:

4.11.) The police would not stop drinking.

In this case, it is not possible to assign alternative phrase structure descriptions to the sentence. This is because all the words play the same grammatical role in the structural description assigned by the grammar, irrespective of the interpretation given the sentence. In particular, the phrase "the police" is the noun phrase associated with the verb phrase "would not stop drinking" on both interpretations. The grammar is unable to indicate the varying role of "the police" to the action "would not stop drinking". Thus, phrase structure grammars cannot always explain the ambiguity underlying a sentence. They do not adequately explain the native speaker's linguistic competence. Chomsky calls ambiguous sentences of the type 4.10.), surface structure ambiguities because we can immediately assign alternative descriptions to the sentences as they stand. On the other hand, he calls ambiguous sentences of type 4.11.), deep structure ambiguities. We shall see shortly why he characterises them in this way.

Chomsky argues that to be explanatorily adequate, a grammar should not only be able to assign structural descriptions to all the sentences in a language but it should be able to capture various native speaker intuitions, like those described above, about the sentences in the language. Chomsky also argues that a native speaker's grammatical knowledge of the language, e.g. word-order rules, can be considered independently of his semantic knowledge of the language, e.g. the meaning of words. He supports his argument by pointing to such meaningless sentences;

4.12.) *Colourless green ideas sleep furiously.[2]

Native speakers of English will generally agree that although sentence 4.12.) is meaningless, it does conform to the grammatical rules of the language. In other words, judgements of grammaticality can be made independently of the meaning of a sentence. It is worth noting in this connection that phrase structure grammars also give us no information about the meaning of a sentence. They tell us how the words are structurally related to each other in the sentence. But it is necessary to have a further set of rules for interpreting this structure in order to derive the meaning of the sentence. For example, we have already discussed a meaningful concept like the subject of the sentence. "Subject" was defined earlier as the noun phrase node that was directly dominated by the sentence node in the structure. Similarly, "object" was defined as the noun phrase node dominated by the verb phrase node. It is important to remember that concepts like "subject" and "object" are not defined by the grammar itself, but by rules that interpret the structures assigned by the grammar. Thus, "subject" and "object" are related also to the native speaker's semantic knowledge. Similarly, the elements of the structural description are grammatical categories, not semantic categories. For example, knowing that a word is a noun tells you little about the meaning of the word. Nouns are grammatical entities which the grammar assigns to various roles in the structural description of the sentence. The linguistic criteria for deciding whether a word is a noun or not, are not based on the word's meaning but on the various positions in which the word can occur in the sentences of the language, i.e. nouns are distributionally defined entities. When we use such terms as "concrete noun" or "abstract noun" we are, in fact, taking that class of words which the grammar defines as a noun and then making an additional semantic classification of the words.

I make these rather detailed comments because it is important to realise that Chomsky's theory of transformational grammar makes no attempt to describe the native speaker's semantic knowledge. The

---

[2]   "*" indicates an ill-formed sentence.

theory is exclusively concerned with describing and explaining the **Syntactic Rules** of the language, i.e. those rules which are concerned with the word-order rules of the language and assign structural descriptions to the sentences of the language. Let us now turn to a more detailed treatment of transformational grammar itself.

We begin by describing Chomsky's proposal for capturing the native speaker's intuitions that sentences can be grouped together in families as we saw on p. 66. Chomsky claims that our intuition that the sentences in a sentence family are somehow related, arises from the fact that they are all derived from the same underlying structure. This does not mean that we can assign the same structure to each of the sentences in a sentence family. Such a procedure would be patently absurd since, although the sentences are somehow related, they are also clearly different sentences. We need some way of capturing both the differences and the similarities between the sentences. Chomsky solves this problem by proposing that each sentence can be assigned two different structural descriptions. He calls these two structural descriptions, the **"surface structure"** and the **"deep structure"** of the sentence, respectively. Thus, sentences in a sentence family are somehow related because they all have the same "deep structure". They are, at the same time, different because they have different "surface structures".

Such a solution to the problem would, of course, be totally vacuous if Chomsky did not provide us with a definition of the "surface structure" and "deep structure" of a sentence plus an explanation of how these two structural descriptions are related. We can get a good idea of what Chomsky means by "deep structure" and "surface structure" by describing what they look like for two of the sentences from the sentence family on p. 66, namely the simple active sentence;

4.5.)   Stephen is eating the cake.

and the corresponding passive form,

4.8.)   The cake is being eaten by Stephen.

According to Chomsky the "surface structures" of these sentences are the same as those that would be assigned by an ordinary phrase structure grammar. These are shown in figure 4.9.:

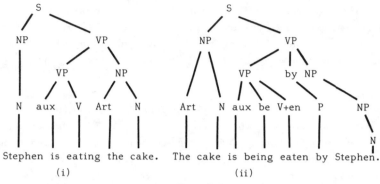

Fig. 4.9.

So far, nothing revolutionary or event unusual is proposed. However, the "deep structure" of these sentences are described as consisting of a phrase structure description plus a "transformational tag". The phrase structure description is identical to that of the simple active sentence in figure 4.9., i). The transformational tag initiates the operation of a particular transformational rule. For example, the deep structure of the passive sentence, "The cake is being eaten by Stephen", consists of the phrase structure of the simple active form of the sentence family, i.e. figure 4.9., i) plus a transformational tag P to instigate the operation of the passive transformational rule. The passive transformational rule is given in Rule 4 below:

$$\textbf{Rule 4: } NP_1\text{--}Aux\text{--}V\text{--}NP_2 \quad \blacktriangleright \quad NP_2\text{--}Aux\text{+}be\text{+}en\text{--}V\text{+}by\text{+}NP_1$$

Notice that rule 4 is unlike rules 1–3 as given in table 4.1. Rules 1–3 expand a single symbol into a series of symbols. However, rule 4 transforms a series of symbols into another series of symbols which both rearranges and adds to the original series. The numbering of the noun phrases in rule 4 enables one to keep track of the two different noun phrases in the transformational process. If you apply rule 4 to the phrase structure as described in figure 4.9. i), you obtain the structure described in figure 4.9. ii), namely the usual passive structure.

There are a number of other transformational rules which act on strings of grammatical symbols, as defined by the "deep" phrase structure, to produce different surface structures. For example, in addition to the passive transformational rule given in rule 4, there are negation transformations, imperative transformations, interrogative transformations and many others. They all operate on the deep structure to produce varying surface structures. The "active" transformational rule is a special case which keeps the surface structure

	Sentence	Transformation
i)	The boy hit the ball	A.
ii)	The ball was hit by the boy	P.
iii)	The boy did not hit the ball.	N.
iv)	Did the boy hit the ball?	Q.
v)	The ball was not hit by the boy.	PN.
vi)	Was the ball hit by the boy?	PQ.
vii)	Did the boy not the ball?	QN.
viii)	Was the ball not hit by the boy?	PQN.

A=Active transformation. P=Passive. Q=Interrogative. N=Negative.

Table 4.2.

of simple active sentences in the same form as their deep phrase structure. Thus, the surface structure and deep structure of "Stephen is eating the cake", are identical except that the deep structure also contains an active transformational tag (A). Table 4.2. gives a listing of sentences which all have the same deep structure excepting the associated transformational tags. Each deep structure is the same as the surface structure associated with the first simple active sentence, "The boy hit the ball". The transformational tags initiate the operation of a rule which transforms the deep structure into the appropriate surface structure.

Deep Structure   Surface Structure

Fig. 4.10.

The diagram in figure 4.10. summarises the nature of the relationship between the deep structure and surface structure of a

71

sentence. As its name suggests, the surface structure describes the structure of the sentence as it is spoken or written. However, this surface structure is derived from the deep structure via the appropriate transformational rules.

Chomsky's transformational grammar can do more than just provide an explanation of the native speaker's intuitions that sentences go together in families. As far as the linguist is concerned, it makes his job slightly easier. Prior to Chomsky's transformational grammar, sentences tended to be described in terms of phrase structure grammars. Thus a different phrase structure had to be written for every different type of sentence structure in the language. By introducing transformational rules, Chomsky did away with the need for describing so many phrase structures. Instead, only a few simple deep phrase structures were required. The transformational component of the grammar did the rest. For example, in table 4.2, traditional phrase structure approaches to describing sentence structure would have required a total of eight different tree structures to distinguish between the eight sentences. However, transformational grammar manages with just one deep phrase structure and three transformational rules. Clearly, transformational grammar is a far more powerful and effective way of describing the rules underlying the sentences of a language.

Transformational grammar is also able to give an account of the ambiguity of such sentences as:

4.11.) The police would not stop drinking.

You will remember from p. 67 that we are able to distinguish at least two different types of ambiguous sentence. The first type which we called surface structure ambiguities could easily be explained by the fact that they could be assigned two different phrase structures. In contrast, deep structure ambiguities, like the sentence above, can only be assigned one surface structure. Chomsky points out that such ambiguities can be explained in terms of the existence of structural representations on two distinct levels for every sentence of the language, namely the deep and surface structures. Deep structure ambiguities like "The police would not stop drinking", occur because a single surface structure can be derived from two different deep structures. That is to say, two sets of transformational rules may operate on two deep structures to produce an identical surface struc-

72

ture. Thus the relationships between "the police" and "would not stop drinking", though indistinguishable at the surface structure level, are indeed distinguishable at the deep structure level because each interpretation of the sentence has two different deep structures. One of these deep structures includes a grammatical symbol representing the person or persons whom the police would not stop drinking. In the transformational process this symbol has been deleted from the structure.

Transformational grammar was so successful in linguistic circles that it was not long before it caught the attention of the psychological world. Chomsky's claim that linguistics is a branch of psychological science also helped to fuel the psychologist's interest. Just as with phrase structure grammars, it was asked if Chomsky's linguistic theory had any psychological validity. We have already seen, that phrase structure grammars do seem to capture some of the linguistic knowledge possessed by native speakers. At least, native speakers were sensitive to the phrase structure of the sentences in the experimental situation in which they were tested. Insofar as, Chomsky's theory includes a phrase structure component then Johnson's results and Garrett at al.'s results can also be regarded as supportive evidence for the psychological reality of transformational grammar.However, what really caught the eye of psychologists was the transformational component of the grammar. The reason for this interest relates to the simplification that transformational grammar introduces to linguistic description. In phrase structure grammars, all the different types of sentences, actives, passives, interrogative, negatives, etc. are assigned different structures. Sentences are difficult to compare in a quantitative way because each has a unique structure. However, in transformational grammar it is possible to compare different sentences more directly because they often derive from the same deep structure. For example, it was suggested that a measure of sentence complexity could be obtained from the number of transformational rules that are necessary to derive the surface structure from the deep structure. Thus, as one moves down the column of sentences in Table 4.2., they become increasingly complex in terms of the number of transformations associated with each sentence. Notice that transformational complexity is not a measure of the length of the sentence. Thus sentence v) is less complex than viii) even though the sentences are of equal length. The notion that transformational grammar could provide a psychological measure of sentence complexity became known as the **Derivational Theory of Complexity** (DTC).

It was not long before the DTC was tested. Here we shall briefly summarise one attempt to evaluate the theory. In many ways, it represents the first sprout from the seed of the new interdisciplinary science that became known as **psycholinguistics**. In 1962, George Miller proposed that an important part of the understanding of a sentence was the derivation of its deep structure. In other words, when a native speaker hears a sentence, in order to understand it properly he must analyse the sentence in terms of its deep structure. Miller's proposal seemed quite reasonable given the importance of deep structure in representing the grammatical relations which are necessary for the interpretation of the sentence. Thus, Miller argued that the more complicated a sentence, as measured by its derivational complexity, i.e. the number of transformations necessary to derive the surface structure from the deep structure, the more difficult it should be to understand. The following experiment was designed to test this hypothesis. Subjects were presented with a piece of paper containing two columns of sentences, with equal numbers of sentences in each column. All the sentences were about different topics and varied in length. The only exception was that one sentence in the first column had the same deep structure as one sentence in the second column, i.e. both sentences came from the same sentence family. Figure 4.11 gives an example that Miller used.

Column 1	Column 2
'	'
'	'
'	'
Joe warned the old woman.	'
'	'
'	The old woman was warned by Joe

Fig. 4.11

The subject's task was to identify these two sentences as quickly and as accurately as possible.

Miller's results were astounding! To understand why, we need to consider Miller's experimental hypothesis. Miller reasoned that the further apart the two matching sentences were, transformationally speaking, the longer it would take to discover that they did indeed match. In other words, Miller assumed that since subjects would analyse sentences in terms of their deep structure they could only decide that two sentences matched when they had discovered that both their deep structures were identical.

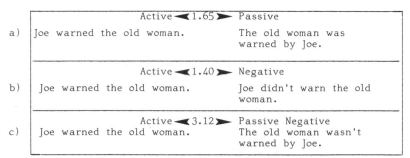

	Active ◄ 1.65 ► Passive	
a)	Joe warned the old woman.	The old woman was warned by Joe.
	Active ◄ 1.40 ► Negative	
b)	Joe warned the old woman.	Joe didn't warn the old woman.
	Active ◄ 3.12 ► Passive Negative	
c)	Joe warned the old woman.	The old woman wasn't warned by Joe.

Table 4.3 (after Miller, 1962)

The length of time needed to do this would depend on the similarity of the two sentences' transformational histories. Table 4.3. summarises some of Miller's results. The numbers in table 4.3. represent the average time taken to identify the two matching sentences in the lists. Thus, the average time taken to identify the Active and Negative forms of a sentence took 1.4 seconds. Interestingly, Miller found that the time taken to match the sentences seemed to be independent of the target sentences used. The important time factor was how the sentences differed transformationally. For example, no matter which pair of sentences were used they would take about 1.40 seconds to identify provided they differed only in terms of the negative transformation. Similarly, if two sentences differed only by a passive transformation they would take 1.65 seconds to identify. This was good evidence for the transformational description of sentences, i.e. that transformations are a psychologically valid concept and can be used to predict people's behaviour. However, the finding that made Miller's experiment so astounding was that transformations appear to be additive in their effect in the matching process. For example, in c) in table 4.3. the two sentences differ by a combination of the negative and passive transformations. A quick mental calculation will reveal that the time taken to match these two sentences, i.e. 3.12 seconds, is approximately the sum of the two transformations taken individually. This result strongly suggested that people do, indeed, analyse sentences by obtaining their deep structures and that they do so by "detransforming" the surface structures in a piecemeal fashion, one transformation at a time.

Miller's experiment inspired a lot of excitement in the psychological world. His results suggested that Chomsky's transformational grammar might provide psychologists with a deep insight into the way in which people understand and produce sentences. Indeed, if Chomsky was to be believed, the theory could provide important insights into the structure of the human mind. During the sixties, the self-styled "psycholinguists" performed numerous experiments to investigate the psychological reality of transformational grammar. However, for the time being we shall leave these industrious psycholinguists to themselves. Having introduced Chomsky's theory and some related evidence, now let us pause to consider what implications it has for our understanding of the development of language and cognition. What are the important insights into the structure of the human mind that Chomsky claims for transformational grammar?

5   DEVELOPMENTAL PSYCHOLINGUISTICS

5.1   Universal Grammar.

One of the most daunting tasks with which the young child is faced, is the learning of the language of his native culture. By the age of twelve months, he is only just beginning to produce his first adult-like words. However, by the age of 3 years, the young toddler has mastered a significant proportion of his native language. In the space of two years, the young child has developed into a linguistically competent individual. Chomsky was well aware that if his theory of transformational grammar was to be an adequate description of the adult speaker's linguistic competence, then quite clearly it should be a grammar that the child can learn. This apparently simple condition of learnability posed Chomsky a number of problems.

To begin with it is important to understand that in learning a language, the child is learning a system of rules. Very often, the sentences that we speak or write have never been spoken or written before. The child cannot learn a language by simply learning all the sentences of the language. Apart from the fact that there are an enormously large number of sentences (perhaps infinite) in a language, a simple rote learning process could not explain how individuals, including children, are able to produce grammatically well-formed sentences which they have never heard before. Neither could such a theory explain how individuals, including children, can recognise that certain utterances are ungrammatical. Clearly, in learning a language the child is learning a system of rules. The rules that he learns he can then use to produce and understand brand new utterances as well as judge the grammaticality of his own and others' utterances. According to Chomsky, these rules are the rules of transformational grammar.

Preliminary Approaches to Language Development

How does the child learn these rules? As we discussed in chapter one, the rules of language vary from one culture to another both in terms of the words and classifications used (semantic rules) and in the syntactic (word-order) rules used. For example, Japanese uses a different syntax to indicate the subject, verb and object of a sentence than does English (see previous chapter). Clearly, if the child is to stand any chance of learning his native language, he must, at the very least, have an opportunity to hear it. Presumably, it is by hearing language that the child is able to notice its regularities and thus learn its rules. The English child learns that the object of the sentence comes after the verb whilst the Japanese child learns that the object comes before the verb. However, this is precisely where Chomsky's problems begin. For you will remember that the rules of transformational grammar are not observable in the surface structure of the sentence. Transformational grammar consists of a set of deep structure rules plus a set of transformational rules. How is the child supposed to learn these rules when they are not directly observable in the utterances he hears? How is the child supposed to infer the rules of the language from the surface structure of the sentence? Furthermore, how does the child know that the rules he is searching for (albeit unconsciously) are a combination of a phrase structure component and a transformational component? What makes the child conceive of linguistic rules in terms of transformational grammar instead of, say, traditional phrase structure rules which are more directly observable?

As if these problems were not enough, Chomsky points to a number of other difficulties that the child faces in learning the syntactic rules of his language. One of Chomsky's achievements in linguistic analysis was to demonstrate that even a grammar as powerful as transformational grammar would have to be enormously complicated in order to describe completely the intricate rules of a spoken natural language. So complicated are natural language rule systems that Chomsky likened their complexity to the theories of advanced theoretical mathematics! What chance then is there for a young child to master such a rule system?

Yet another difficulty for the child, is that adults often fail to speak in well-formed grammatical sentences. Their linguistic performances tend to be characterised by false starts, slips of the tongue and half-completed sentences; all of which make the grammatical structure of the sentence less transparent and so more difficult for the child to decipher. Learning a transformational grammar, given the bad working conditions, would seem an almost impossible task.

Chomsky's solution to these problems is fundamental to his whole theoretical position. He proposes that the young infant comes to the language learning situation, innately equipped to learn the language of his culture. This innate knowledge directs him to look for special types of rules underlying the language that he hears, namely the rules of transformational grammar. Furthermore, the knowledge enables the child to infer the rules even when the samples of speech that he hears are not complete sentences.

A proposal which puts forward the idea that children come into the world already having some knowledge of their native tongue seems counter-intuitive to what we know about children's language development. We know that it takes several years for children to become effective language users but more importantly we know that any innate linguistic knowledge could not be specific to any particular language. A Japanese child brought up by English parents will learn English just as quickly as a normal English child. Chomsky's proposal for the existence of innate linguistic knowledge must be more general. In fact, Chomsky calls the innate linguistic knowledge possessed by young infants, **Universal Grammar.** It is a grammar which underlies all the languages of the world. That is to say, all the languages of the world conform to the rules of this grammar which consists of a **phrase structure component** and a **transformational component.** The problem is to describe just exactly what this grammar might look like. Given the wide variety of languages in the world, and their corresponding differences, it is difficult to imagine a universal transformational component or a universal phrase structure component. At the very least, they must be extremely general. Yet Chomsky claims that this knowledge is crucial to the child in the language learning process.

What evidence is there that such a grammar exists? Unfortunately, the only answer we can give at present is, "Precious little". However, there are some interesting facts that linguists have uncovered in their mad rush to discover the Universal Grammar. For example, all languages seem to utilise structures which encode subject, verb and object relations. Furthermore, the order of operation of transformational rules on the deep structure of sentences does not vary much from one language to the next. Passive, Negative and Interrogative transformations, for example, operate on the deep

structure in the same cyclic way irrespective of the language considered. However, perhaps the most persuasive evidence that there
are innate constraints on the linguistic structure that people use can
be seen if we consider how different languages order subject, verb
and object in their sentences. Table 5.1. gives a summary of the
world's different basic language structures.

VO-Languages		OV-Languages	
SVO	35%	SOV	44%
VSO	19%		
VOS	2%		

Table 5.1.

The table divides the world's languages into two broad classes; languages whose syntactic rules place the verb before the object, like English; and languages whose syntactic rules place the
object before the verb, like Japanese. (It should be noted that languages vary in the extent to which they use syntax to indicate the
role of the word in a sentence. Many languages, e.g. Turkish, use
inflections on word endings to indicate the word's role). However,
notice that of six possible S, V and O structures – all the permuta-
tions of S, V and O – only four are actually found in the languages
of the world. This suggests a genetic constraint on the human ability to structure sentences. Chomsky interprets this constraint as
part of the individual's innate linguistic knowledge which makes up
Universal Grammar.

Chomsky's view that adult linguistic competence derives from
innate, and specifically innate **linguistic** knowledge, parallels his
view that language is an independent capacity of the human mind.
He argues that the knowledge underlying linguistic skills is not a
mere reflection of general intellectual knowledge. Linguistic skills,
and in particular syntactic skills, require a unique kind of knowledge that cannot be acquired through a general learning process.
This unique linguistic knowledge must be an innate characteristic of
the human mind. By characterising the native speaker's linguistic
competence in this way, Chomsky isolates linguistic knowledge from
other forms of knowing. In effect, any relationship between language

and thought is denied, at least as far as syntactic knowledge is concerned. And in a developmental context, language acquisition is seen as governed exclusively by maturational factors and a modicum of linguistic experience.

5.2 Rules in Child Language

The dominance of transformational grammar, during the late fifties and sixties, encouraged students of child language to investigate the process of rule acquisition which Chomsky proposed children must undergo during the first few years of life. That children learn their language by acquiring a system of rules, was already pretty well-established. For example, it has been well-known since the early diary studies of children's language in the nineteenth century that children make certain kinds of linguistic "mistakes" which can only be explained in terms of a developing rule system. Consider the verbs "hold" and "fall". In the adult language, these verbs are irregular, i.e. their past tenses are not formed in the regular way by inflecting with an "-ed". Instead, the forms "held" and "fell" are used respectively. Sometime during the beginning of their third year children will begin to use these irregular past tense forms in appropriate situations. However, a little later in the year, a curious retrograde step seems to be taken by the child; the forms "held" and "fell" appear to drop out of the child's vocabulary only to be replaced by the incorrect substitutes, "holded" and "falled". A similar phenomenon is observed for nouns with irregular plurals like "feet" and "sheep" which are replaced by the incorrect substitutes "foots" and "sheeps" respectively.

During the same period that the child begins to make these "mistakes", he also begins to use the "-ed" morpheme in a productive fashion. That is, the child starts uttering the past tenses of verbs he has only ever previously used in the present tense. For example, he might now use "walked" whereas previously he only used "walk". One way we can explain this development is by appealing to the notion that the child has discovered the rule for forming the past tense of verbs. He has done so by reflecting on his own use of verb forms in different situations as well as the adult's usage. The child has learnt that you form the past tense of the verb simply by adding "-ed". The ubiquity with which the child suddenly starts to use the past tense morpheme in a productive fashion makes this argument a compelling one. However, this does not rule out the possibility that the sudden growth in new past tense forms is a consequence of the sudden imitation of adult usages. Just because a child has not produced a particular past tense form before does not mean he has not heard it used and so remembered it for using at a later date. However, this interpretation of the emergence of the past tense morpheme is rendered less likely by the data reported on irregular verbs and nouns. It is extremely unlikely that the young child has ever heard the verb forms "holded" and "falled" used before. Consequently, we cannot explain their use in terms of an imitation model. On the other hand, we can explain these "mistaken" usages in terms of an overgeneralisation of the newly learnt rule system. The child learns that one forms the past tense of a verb by adding "ed". This knowledge is then applied indiscriminately over the whole spectrum of verbs, including those verbs whose irregular past tenses have already been learnt through simple imitation. In fact, it will take the child a good few months to discover the limits of his new rule and so begin to use the irregular past tense correctly again.

The child's tendency to look for rules in his language would seem so powerful that it obliterates even those aspects of his language which he has learnt correctly by imitation. The child's linguistic "mistakes", far from representing retrograde steps in the process of language development, would seem to signify important progress; namely, progressive access to the rule system of the language. However, the kind of rules which we have discussed so far in this section are morphemic rules which relate to the child's semantic system. They are rules which enable the child to change systematically, the meaning of a word, e.g. from singular to plural. However, this type of rule constitutes only a part of the adult linguistic system. Other rules like syntactic rules and pragmatic rules are needed to provide a complete account of language. Transformational grammar is concerned solely with syntactic rules. It is no accident then that child language researchers, under the influence of the Chomskyian revolution, concentrated their attention on the child's acquisition of word-order rules. A consideration of morphemic rules, like those discussed above, and pragmatic rules was left to one side. The appealing but difficult question of how the child learns the syntactic rules of his language, as described by Chomsky, completely captivated the minds and energies of child language researchers. In fact, in accordance with their predominant interest in

language development, they even coined a new name for their interdisciplinary science. They called it **Developmental Psycholinguistics.**

5.3 Pivot Grammars

Chomsky had proposed that children come to the language learning
situation with some innate linguistic knowledge which they use to
discover the specific syntactic rules of their own language. How then
does this knowledge manifest itself in the child's early language
usage? Clearly, if we are to investigate the emergence of word-order
rules in child language we need to investigate those utterances in
which the child combines words that he already knows. In the course
of normal language development, this does not happen until towards
the end of the child's second year. Prior to this time, the child's
language consists exclusively of single-word utterances often combined with gestures. Such language is clearly not amenable to syntactic analysis. However, once the child reaches the two-word stage,
we can begin to investigate if there is any organisation in the way
he puts his words together. In the present context, we can investigate if there are any constraints on the ordering of words in a
child's utterance. Here is an example of a fairly typical exchange
between a mother and her two-year-old child.

> Child: What's that?
> Mother: That's daddy's pipe.
> Child: Daddy pipe.
> Mother: Mmm.
> Child: Daddy gone.
> Mother: Yes, that's right, daddy's gone to work.
> Child: Gone work.

By the age of two years, many children have a vocabulary of
several hundred words. The number of possible two-word combinations
is therefore immense. Try calculating the number of possible two-
word combinations with a vocabulary of just ten words. (The answer
is 90). The question that intrigued developmental psycholinguists
was: Do children produce all possible combinations or is there some
kind of constraint on the type of two-word utterances produced?

A number of studies of different children in the two-word stage
of language development found that not all possible combinations
seemed to be used by the children. In particular, their vocabularies
seemed to consist of some words which occurred frequently and often

in a particular position in the combination while other words occurred a lot less frequently and had no preferable position in the combination. This finding that children's vocabularies seemed to consist of two different types of words, as defined by frequency and position, was a common finding for almost every study of two-word utterances in the child language literature, irrespective of cultural or socio-economic background. If some words are used more frequently than others then the number of two-word combinations observed will be less than when each word in the vocabulary is used equally frequently. However, frequency of occurrence in itself tells us nothing about the word-order rules that might constrain the number of two-word combination. In this respect, the finding that the frequent words also had a privileged position of occurrence was of more interest. For example, if some words only occur in the first position of a two-word combination this suggests that child not only has knowledge about the word itself, but also knowledge about where that word can occur when combined with other words, i.e. syntactic knowledge. Simultaneously, a constraint on a word's position in a two-word utterance would limit the number of total possible two-word combinations.

The problem facing developmental psycholinguists was to find some way of formulating this constraint on the child's two-word combinations, such that they could predict which combinations the child could produce and which combinations he could not produce. At first sight, this problem is relatively easy to solve. If we focus exclusively on word-order constraints then for two-word utterances any single word may be subject to any one of the following three limitations:

1. The word occurs only in the initial position of the combination.
2. The word occurs only in the final position of the combination.
3. The word can occur in either position.

Logically, these are the only three possibilities for constraining the position of a word in a two-word utterance. In essence, they divide up the two-year old's vocabulary into three syntactic categories such that each of the child's words belongs to one and only one of the three categories. Notice that these categories are syntactic categories, not semantic categories, since they are defined solely in terms of the word's position in the utterance and not in terms of its meaning. In this respect, they resemble the grammatical categories like noun, verb, adjective, etc. which we discussed in chapter 4. The finding that certain frequent words in the two-year old's vocabulary have privileged positions of occurrence, i.e. they tended to occur in the initial position or the final position of the utterance, and that infrequent words could occur in either position; suggested that the three grammatical categories outlined above might be a good way of describing the constraints on a two-year old's two-word utterances.

Braine (1963) was amongst the first developmental psycholinguists to describe the rules underlying two-word speech. Braine based his theory on the data he collected from three children, Gregory, Andrew and Steven who had just entered the period of multi-word utterances. It is important to remember that his analysis was based purely on the distribution of the children's words in their two-word utterances, i.e. whether the word occurred first or second. Braine was not concerned with the meaning of the children's utterances. Gregory's, Andrew's and Steven's two-word utterances also showed the classical pattern found by other researchers; a small set of words occurred very frequently whilst the majority of the words occurred infrequently. However, Braine noticed that corresponding to the frequent/infrequent distinction was a clear-cut word-order effect. In particular, the frequent words seemed to divide into two classes of words. One class of word only ever occurred in the initial position in the utterances whilst the other class only occurred in the final position. Furthermore, he noted that words from these two classes never occurred alone, i.e. they were never used as single-word utterances. Neither did the words from each class ever occur together in the utterances. The frequent words always and only occurred in combination with a word from the infrequent group of words, all of which could occur in any position in the utterance. Because of their privileged status in two-word utterances, Braine called this small but frequent group of words, the **Pivot class**. The Pivot class itself then consisted of two sub-classes, **initial pivots** and **final pivots**. The large but infrequent group of words in the child's vocabulary was called the **Open class**. Words from the Open class also occurred as single-word utterances.

Preliminary Approaches to Language Development

The division of the child's vocabulary into the three grammatical classes together with the order information for each of the classes enabled Braine to write a simple grammar for the three children's utterances. The rules of the grammar are summarised in table 5.2 below.

Rule 1.	$U \rightarrow P_1 + 0$
Rule 2.	$U \rightarrow 0 + P_2$
Rule 3.	$U \rightarrow 0 + 0$
U = Utterance	0 = Open class word
P_1 = Initial Pivot	P_2 = Final Pivot

Table 5.2.

There are three different utterance types. Two types consist of an initial or final pivot combined with an open class word. The third type consists of two open class words. These rules provide us with a theory for predicting what the child can and cannot say. They set constraints on the possible two-word combinations that the child might produce. The most important of these constraints is that two pivot words can never occur together in the same utterance. Table 5.3. gives a sample of some two-word utterances produced by one of the children, Andrew. The table is organised such that different utterance types are placed in their respective columns.

On the basis of the rules given in table 5.2. and the analysis provided by table 5.3. you might like to predict what other two-word utterances Andrew should be able to produce. In any case, notice how the utterances of table 5.3. conform to the rules laid down in table 5.2.

The advantage of describing the child's two-word utterances in this way are two-fold. First, Pivot grammar provides us with a description of the child's early linguistic competence that explains how the child can use language in a productive way, i.e. how the child can come to say things which he has never heard said before. Suppose one day the child adds an extra word to his pivot class. He may do so on the basis of hearing an adult using the word. This pivot word can then be used in combination with all the child's open class words which may number several hundred. In other words,

ANDREW		
$P_1 + 0$	$0 + P_2$	$0 + 0$
All broke	Boot off	Papa away
All fix	Water off	Pants change
I see	Airplane by	Dry pants
I sit	Siren by	
No bed	Mail come	
No down	Mama come	
More car	Hot in there	
More sing	Milk in there	
Hi Calico		
Hi Mama		
Other bib		
Other milk		

Table 5.3.

learning just one new pivot word enables the child to produce several hundred new two-word utterances. Secondly, the division of the child's vocabulary into three distinct grammatical categories is reminiscent of the grammatical categories that are used in full blown adult language. McNeill (1970) suggested that the pivot/open distinction might be the first primitive differentiation of the language's grammatical categories. Thus the pivot class may further differentiate into one set of categories, e.g. noun, adjective, article, whilst the open class differentiates into another non-overlapping set, e.g. verb, adverb, preposition. The characterisation of child language in terms of pivot grammar seemed to offer many exciting possibilities in understanding the process of language development. And all this without reference to the meaning of the child's words.

However, the pivot grammar approach was doomed to failure. There were a number of reasons for this outcome, some internal to the grammar itself, and other extraneous reasons. To begin with, the grammar did not sufficiently constrain the number of possible combinations of two-word utterances. That is, pivot grammar predicted that the child would produce certain combinations which he was never heard to produce, e.g. I pants ($P_1 + 0$) or Broke come ($0 + P_2$) (see Table 5.3). Thus, pivot grammar failed to capture adequately the two-year-old's linguistic competence. Secondly, Braine's clear-cut definition of the two pivot classes of words does not seem to hold for other children whose two-word utterances have been similarly analysed. That is, it was difficult to find words in other children's vocabularies which fulfilled all the criteria that Brain used for defining the pivot classes. For example, sometimes supposed pivot words would occur in combination with each other, or occur alone, or even change their position in the utterance. Furthermore, a closer analysis of Braine's own data for Andrew (which is not included in table 5.3.) reveals the existence of pivot-like words which change their position. Pivot grammar was turning out to be an idealisation of the data on two-word utterances; an idealisation which did not match up to reality.

Even McNeill's speculation about the pivot and open classes being the first primitive differentiation of grammatical categories on the way to full blown adult categories turned out to be wrong. A brief perusal of table 5.3. will reveal that the pivot and open classes consist of a wide variety of grammatical categories as defined by the adult grammar. For example, the pivot classes consist of pronouns, adjectives, demonstratives, prepositions, verbs, etc. whilst the open class consists of nouns, prepositions, verbs, adjectives, etc. Clearly these are not non-overlapping classes such that pivots will differentiate into one set of grammatical categories whilst open class words will differentiate into a distinct set. Language development, like life, is not quite that straightforward.

Finally, the pivot and open classes do not seem to describe adequately the two-year old's knowledge of grammatical categories. The two-year old seems to have a more sophisticated knowledge of grammatical categories than Braine's analysis gives him credit for. For example, Bowerman's (1973) analysis of two Finnish children's two-word utterances suggests that they had a mastery of more than the three pivot and open classes. Some initial pivots only occurred before certain types of open class words. For example, the initial pivot "tässä" (meaning "here") only occurred before nouns whilst the proper name "Rina" only occurred before verbs. Such priveleges of occurrence can only be explained if the child has some knowledge of the distinction between a verb and a noun and the other open class words. Otherwise, the child could have no justification for not combining "Rina" and "tässä" with any of the open class words. This suggested that the open class of words was not the undifferentiated class that Braine initially supposed. Children's two-word utterances would appear to contain more adult-like grammatical categories than the wholly unadult-like pivot/open grammar gives them credit for.

5.4   Meaning and Context

Pivot grammars were an important first attempt at trying to describe children's two-word utterances in terms of an ordered system of rules. They combined the child's capacity for the classification of words into grammatical categories with his ability to use language productively; both important hallmarks of any realistic account of child language. We have seen how pivot grammars first emerged in the context of the new transformational approach to describing language. Yet, surprisingly, pivot grammars possessed none of the unique characteristics which made transformational grammar so successful, i.e. deep structures and transformational rules. Pivot grammars concentrated exclusively on assigning surface structure descriptions to children's two-word utterances. In this respect, they emulated the traditional phrase structure descriptions of adult language. Proponents of pivot grammar were thus faced not only with the internal inconsistencies of their own theory but also the problem of reconciling their descriptions in a developmental context with the currently more acceptable transformational approach.

In the late sixties, evidence emerged to suggest that pivot grammar was not only wrong but that it could not possibly have been right. The paradigm switch which brought about this "discovery" stemmed from a growing dissatisfaction among developmental psycholinguists, that the recent preoccupation with word-order rules in two-word utterances gave a too narrow picture of the processes involved in early language development. For example, it is found that children entering the two-word stage also have a rapidly growing vocabulary; the meanings of the words they use seem to be undergoing subtle changes; they start using language for a much greater variety of purposes than hitherto; and last but not least, their intellectual and social development is proceeding at a phenomenal rate. Child language researchers felt that such developments were equally worthy of their attention as word-order rules and, furthermore, that a broader study of the child's linguistic, intellectual and social development might provide a deeper insight into the child's acquistion of syntactic rules.

Preliminary Approaches to Language Development

Initially criticism centred on the notion that it is possible to discover the constraints on two-word combinations by a purely distributional analysis of the words in a child's corpus of two-word utterances. Braine had tried to discover the word-order rules underlying two-word speech in this way and failed. You will remember that one of the reasons for this failure was that pivot grammar predicted that the child would produce more two-word combinations than he was actually heard to produce. Thus, from Table 5.3., we would expect Andrew to be able to produce utterances like "I Pants" and "Broke Come". These are both perfectly grammatical combinations as defined by the Pivot Grammar. Yet Andrew was never heard to produce these utterances. Of course, we as adults are able to produce an almost infinite variety of sentences. Yet we would be unlikely to judge a grammar of adult language wrong just because it predicted the well-formedness of certain word strings that we had never uttered. Only if the grammar predicted that certain strings of words were ungrammatical yet we still uttered those word strings, judging them to be grammatical, would we reject the grammar. In pivot grammar terms, the combination of an initial and final pivot in the same utterance disproves the grammar. The non-occurrence of utterances like "I Pants" and "Broke come" does not disprove the grammar, as such, even though the grammar predicts their possible occurrence. Nevertheless, the non-occurrence of combinations like those above prompted researchers to speculate what kind of constraints might prevent the child from producing them.

Intuitively, it seemed clear that the child refrained from using the non-occurring combinations because they were not meaningful to him. Most of the two-word combinations that children produce seem well-fitted to the context in which they are used and adults have little trouble putting their own interpretations on two-word utterances. Often adults will even provide expansions of the child's previous utterance as a confirmation that they have understood what the child has said or alternatively to question the child's meaning. Table 5.4. presents some typical expansions of child speech by mothers.

Child	Mother
Baby highchair	Baby is in the highchair
Mommy eggnog	Mommy had her eggnog
Eve lunch	Eve is having lunch
Mommy sandwich	Mommy'll have a sandwich
Sat wall	He sat on the wall
Throw Daddy	Throw it to Daddy
Pick glove	Pick the glove up

Source: Brown and Bellugi, 1964.

Table 5.4.

Clearly, the child's two-word combinations are open to other interpretations. For example, "Eve lunch" might be expanded into "Eve is going to have lunch" or "Eve has had lunch". However, this particular two-word utterance was uttered by Eve at 12 noon whilst she was eating her lunch. The context in which the utterance is used enables the parent (or researcher for that matter) to disambiguate the utterance and provide the relevant expansion.

Once we start looking at two-word utterances from the perspective of the child's intended meaning we can see why the pivot grammar approach was destined to fail. Pivot grammar descriptions explicitly took no account of what the child meant by his utterance yet our intuitions convince us that it is the child's intended meaning that restricts the word combinations used by the child, rather than an abstract syntactic rule system. The problem was to formalise these intuitions into a set of rules which would enable us, in the spirit of pivot grammar, to predict which utterances would or would not be produced by the child.

Bloom (1970) was among the first to attempt the mammoth task of describing children's two-word utterances such that their intended meanings might be captured in a formal rule system. Bloom's work represents a turning point in child language research where meaning and context first became important tools in the researcher's conceptual repertoire. Instead of just collecting a corpus of two-word utterances, researchers began to take notes of the ongoing context and jot down spontaneous expansions of the children's utterances like those in Table 5.4. Utterances were still subjected to distributional analysis but within the context of the child's intended meaning. The outcome of any distributional analysis of two-word utterances should not only set meaningful constraints on possible two-word combinations but it should also provide a basis for describing and distinguishing the meanings conveyed in two-word utterances.

Of particular relevance is Bloom's observation of her daughter Kathryn's utterance of the two-word combination "Mommy Sock". This utterance was spoken on two separate occasions in a single day. In terms of a pivot grammar description, the utterance "Mommy Sock" would be a type 3 description (see Table 5.3). i.e. it consists of two open class words (O + O). However, Bloom noted that on the two occasions that Kathryn used the combinations, she seemed to mean something different each time. Bloom's transcriptions describe the different contexts in these terms:

Kathryn picked up her mother's sock.
Mother was putting Kathryn's sock on Kathryn.

In the first of these contexts an adult might very well provide the expansion, "Yes, that's right. It's mommy's sock". In other words, the adult interprets the child's utterance as signalling a relation of possession, i.e. the sock belonging to mommy. In the second context, an adult would provide a different expansion: "That's right, Mommy is putting on your sock". The adult interprets the child as signalling a subject-object relation rather than a possessor-possessed relation. Thus, the single two-word utterance "Mommy sock" seemed to be used by Kathryn to convey two completely different meanings.

Bloom argues that a grammar of two-word utterances should be able to capture these differences by assigning different structures to the alternative interpretations. (You may recognise that Chomsky used the same argument with respect to deep structure ambiguities). Pivot grammar does not assign different structures to the alternative interpretations. The same "O + O" description would be used in each case. Bloom set about writing a grammar that would enable her to describe ambiguous utterances like "Mommy Sock" with different structures. She wanted her descriptions to capture the meaningful differences between utterances as well as the word-order constraints. The most obvious conceptual tool to use for this purpose was trans-formational grammar. The paradigm of transformational grammar provided tools for syntactic analysis. It also provided structural descriptions which were the starting point for an interpretation of the sentence's meaning, i.e. the deep structure. The ingredients were correct. They just needed modifying a little to cope with the special characteristics of two-word speech.

In addition to the possessor-possessed and subject-object relations already interpreted from Kathryn's speech, Bloom found two other relational interpretations frequently justified. These were:

Subject-locative

e.g. Sweater chair (Kathryn puts her sweater on the chair).

Attributive

e.g. Party hat (Kathryn is picking up a hat for parties).

A Grammar for Kathryn

A. Phrase Structure Rules.

1. $S_1 \longrightarrow$ Nom. + (Ng) + $\begin{Bmatrix} NP \\ VP \end{Bmatrix}$

2. $S_2 \longrightarrow$ Pivot + N

3. $VP \longrightarrow V + \begin{Bmatrix} NP \\ Part \end{Bmatrix}$

4. $NP \longrightarrow$ (Adj.) + N

5. $Nom \longrightarrow \begin{Bmatrix} N \\ Dem. \end{Bmatrix}$

B. Transformations

1. $T_{placement}$ (optional) $\begin{Bmatrix} Adj. \\ Prep \end{Bmatrix} + N \longrightarrow N + \begin{Bmatrix} Adj. \\ Prep \end{Bmatrix}$

2. $T_{reduction}$ (obligatory) a) $X + Ng + Y \longrightarrow Ng + Y$
   b) $X_1 + X_2 + X_3 \longrightarrow X_i + X_j$
   (where $1 \leqslant i \leqslant j \leqslant 3$).

C. Lexicon Feature Rules.

   i)   Only animate nouns occur before verbs.

   ii) Animate nouns never occur after Nom or after adjectives.

   iii) Any noun can occur after a preposition.

   iv) Pivots include Hi, Oh, thank you, O.K.

Source: Bloom (1970)

Table 5.5.

All in all then, Bloom identified four different types of relations which her grammar should distinguish in addition to capturing the usual word-order constraints on two-word utterances. Table 5.5. provides a summary of the grammar that Bloom wrote to describe the two-word utterances of her daughter Kathryn.

Many of the symbols and conventions in this grammar will already be familiar to you from the section on phrase structure grammars earlier in this chapter. However, a number of usages are new and need explaining. First you will notice that the grammar, unlike phrase structure grammar, contains a transformational component. It is, therefore, a simple transformational grammar of child language with deep structures and transformational rules. There are also a set of Lexicon Feature Rules which specify non-syntactic constraints on two-word combinations. Thus (i) indicates that only animate nouns i.e. nouns describing objects that can move, can occur before verbs. This is a constraint couched in terms of the word's meaning and represents an important step away from purely distributional criteria. In the set of phrase structure rules, the symbol "(Ng)" stands for negative indicating a word like "no" or "not" in the deep structure. The symbol "Dem" stands for demonstrative and includes words like "this", "there" or "that". Parentheses "( )" indicate that the element to the right of the arrow is an optional component of the rewrite rule. Thus, in rule 1 "(Ng)" indicates that "Ng" may or may not be included in the expansion of the "S_1" node. Braces "$\{\ \}$" indicate that one of the elements contained within the brackets must be chosen in the rewrite expansion. Thus, in rule 5, Nom must be rewritten as N or Dem. Otherwise, the phrase structure rules operate in exactly the same fashion as the ones already discussed in chapter 4. You will notice that there are no lexical rules. These are excluded for purely practical reasons. The child's vocabulary at this time will contain several hundred different words. The reader is referred to Bloom's original account for the grammatical classification of Kathryn's vocabulary.

The transformational component of the grammar is interesting for several reasons. First, it represents the earliest attempt to describe children's two-word utterances with transformational rules. This may seem somewhat surprising given that Chomsky had first formulated his theory more than 13 years earlier. Secondly, the nature of the rules themselves are interesting. The first rule, B.1., is a prototypical transformational rule which simply reorders a deep structure to produce an alternative surface structure. In Kathryn's grammar, the application of this rule is optional, i.e. sometimes Kathryn ordered the specified string in one way and at other times she would reverse it. Notice though that the transformational rule B.1. is defined in terms of syntactic categories (N, Adj., Prep.) and in itself has no semantic component. This is a general characteristic of transformational rules: They are defined purely in syntactic terms and have no effect or relation to the meaning of the utterance. All meaning relations can be obtained from the deep structure. This is also true of transformational rule B.2. which plays a rather peculiar role in Kathryn's grammar.

Bloom was exclusively interested in writing a grammar for Kathryn's two-word utterances. Yet she found that the phrase structure rules necessary for capturing the deep structure relations of Kathryn's corpus of utterances occasionally resulted in structures with three terminal elements. In other words, the deep structure component of the grammar was also producing descriptions for three-word utterances. (We will discuss such an example shortly). Bloom needed some way of retaining these descriptions since they enabled her to capture the underlying relations in Kathryn's sentences. Yet the grammar was only intended to describe Kathryn's two-word utterances. Bloom concluded that she needed a reduction transformation which would remove one of the terminal elements from those deep structures which contain three terminal elements; thereby retaining the richness of Kathryn's deep structures, yet preserving the surface structure constraint that the utterance be only two words long. Thus transformational rule B.2a) always removes the first element from a string of three terminal elements when the middle element belongs to the Negative category. B.2b) operates on all other three element strings, removing one of the elements, but otherwise preserving their order.

Bloom justified the inclusion of these reduction transformations on the grounds that the structures underlying Kathryn's two-word utterances were richer than her two-word combinations suggested. Furthermore, the disparity between surface structure complexity and deep structure complexity could be explained in terms of a memory limitation on the number of words that Kathryn could combine. This memory limitation was nothing to do with Kathryn's linguistic competence as such, but a more general psychological constraint on the child's performance skills. The reduction transformation was a necessary accommodation of the child's linguistic competence to her psychological performance capacities, in this case memory span.

Having described the grammar, let us now consider how we can actually use it to describe Kathryn's utterances. In order to demonstrate the power of this type of description in relation to pivot grammars we will present an analysis that the grammar provides for the two alternative interpretations of the utterance "Mommy Sock". First, consider the subject–object interpretation, i.e. "That's right, Mommy is putting on your sock". Table 5.6. gives the rule–by–rule derivation plus the resultant tree structure.

Subject–Object Interpretation of "Mommy Sock"

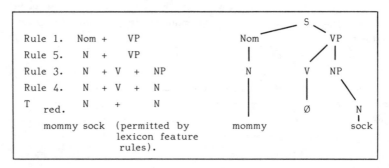

Rule 1.	Nom +	VP
Rule 5.	N +	VP
Rule 3.	N + V +	NP
Rule 4.	N + V +	N
T red.	N +	N
	mommy sock	(permitted by lexicon feature rules).

Table 5.6

Notice that the phrase structure component produces a terminal string containing three elements, N + V + N. This instigates the operation of the reduction transformation B.2b) which in this case eliminates the terminal element underlying the verb (labelled Ø). The deep structure which describes the terminal string N + V + N is thus transformed into the surface string N + N. However, it is the deep structure, as depicted in the tree diagram of Table 5.6, which shows the underlying roles of the two nouns in the combination. One of the nouns (sock) belongs to the verb phrase and so is interpreted as the object in the utterance. The other noun (mommy) is derived directly from the sentence node and so is interpreted as the subject of the sentence. These definitions of subject and object correspond to the rules for interpreting phrase structures given on p. 59. Without the rich deep structure assigned to this two–word utterance, we would have been unable to formulate so clearly the subject-object relation between "Mommy" and "sock".

Table 5.7 provides the equivalent description for the alternative interpretation of "Mommy sock", i.e. "That's right, it's mommy's sock". In this case, no transformational rule operates. The surface structure is identical with the deep structure. Again we have a terminal string of two nouns, but this time the nouns are assigned different roles in the deep structure from the nouns in Table 5.6. In particular, the second noun "sock" is not part of a verb phrase and so cannot be an object in the utterance.

Possessor-Possessed Interpretation of "Mommy Sock".

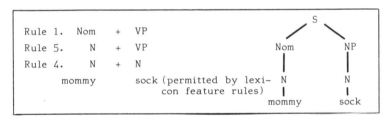

Table 5.7.

Thus Bloom succeeded in assigning two different structural descriptions to the utterance "Mommy Sock" in a way that captures our intuitions about the different meanings of the utterance. Furthermore, she was able to do so by using concepts from transformational grammar, e.g. deep structures and transformational rules. The link between descriptions of adult language and child language was thus forged. Bloom's achievement was considerable. Not only did she succeed in specifying the constraints on possible two-word combinations from a syntactic perspective, but she also ensured that the grammar predicted utterances which were **meaningful** in relation to the child's world. That is not to say that Bloom provided us with a theory of the semantic rules of child language. The grammar in Table 5.5 provides us with very little semantic information concerning Kathryn's vocabulary. However, Bloom did identify four important meaning relations that could be frequently interpreted from the child's utterances; namely, possessor-possessed, subject-object, subject-locative and attributive. The grammar was able to assign distinct structures to each of these relations, and so provide us with a tool for better understanding Kathryn's two-word combinations.

The use of meaning and context in describing two-word utterances represented a critical turning point in the study of child language. From Bloom's study onwards, all work on child language has taken into account the intended meaning of the child's utterance as derived from the ongoing context. This is as true of studies of syntactic development as it is of studies of semantic or pragmatic development. Developmental psycholinguists were quickly convinced that the assignment of words to grammatical classes should not be made on the basis of distributional evidence alone. The meaning of the word had an important role to play.

5.5 A Language Acquisition Device

> Typically, in all of the cultures we have examined, there is a period of babbling ending somewhere around 18 months of age. Overlapping this period is a stage of single-word utterances, followed by a stage of two-word utterances at around 18-24 months. The two-word stage is often quite brief, but its structural and semantic properties appear to be universal. There is no a priori reason why child speech, at a certain stage, should be limited to utterances of two words in length, for children can babble much longer strings of sounds. The universality of this phase suggests the maturation of a "language acquisition device" with a fairly fixed programme span for utterances at the start. (Slobin, 1970, p. 176).

Slobin's "language acquisition device" is a concept resembling Chomsky's "Universal Grammar"; namely, the innate knowledge that enables young children to learn the language of their native culture. However, Slobin has developed the concept still further to include not only innate syntactic knowledge but also innate semantic knowledge as well. Like the syntactic component of Universal Grammar, innate semantic knowledge is not intended to provide information unique to the young child's native language. It does not provide information about the meaning of a word in the language, e.g. which objects the word "lemon" refers to or whether a "lemon" is classified as a "fruit" or "vegetable". Rather it provided the child with knowledge about the kind of meaningful things that can be uttered in any language, be it English, Japanese, Russian or Swahili. For example, Bloom noted that her daughter Kathryn produced just four different meaningful relations with her two-word utterances, i.e. the relations of possession, attribution, agent–object and subject–location. The appearance of these four meaning relations in Kathryn's speech can be seen as a stage in the maturation of a "language acquisition device" or LAD. Continued maturation of the LAD will reveal an increasing number of meaning relations in the child's utterances as well as an increasing sophistication of the child's syntactic skills.

Bloom's description of Kathryn's two–word utterances provided developmental psycholinguists with a characterisation of a particular stage in the maturation of one child's LAD. A complete description of the child's syntactic skills was combined with a specification of the child's semantic skills. The LAD clearly prompted the child to invent a set of transformational rules and deep structures rather than simply a set of phrase structure rules. Furthermore, the child seemed guided in her creation of meaningful relations. Otherwise, why should she continually encode just the four stated relations in exclusion of a multitude of others? Bloom's findings neatly fitted the notion that the stages in a child's language development reflect a gradual unfolding of an innate LAD. Developmental psycholinguistics seemed, at last, to be on a promising and fruitful path. The obvious next step was to test the universality of Bloom's findings, uncovering those aspects of Kathryn's syntactic and semantic knowledge which were specific to English and Kathryn herself and those aspects which had a more general, universal character.

5.6 Transformational Complexity and Meaning

In fact a rather different path was taken. To understand the reasons for the shift in direction we need to take a brief excursion outside the field of developmental psycholinguistics to the fields of "adult" psycholinguistics and linguistics itself. By the end of the sixties, Chomsky's reign of influence was beginning to wane in psychological circles. After a burst of experiments which suggested that Chomsky's transformational grammar had some psychological reality, evidence began to emerge to the contrary. Typical of such evidence were the findings of an experiment conducted by Slobin in 1966. Slobin gave his subjects a Picture Evaluation Task to perform i.e. subjects were presented with both a picture and a sentence, and asked to judge whether the sentence was true or false in relation to the picture. Slobin used both active and passive sentences like;

5.1) The girl hit the boy.
5.2) The boy was hit by the girl.

and replicated the traditional finding that passives take longer to evaluate than actives (see chapter four). However, Slobin incorporated an interesting variation into his experimental design. He introduced a number of active and passive pairs whose meaningfulness cannot be maintained when the grammatical subject and object are swopped. Sentences 5.3) and 5.4) are examples of such constructions.

5.3) The girl watered the flowers.
5.4) The flowers were watered by the girl.

If the grammatical subjects and objects are reversed the sentences become meaningless except in some fantasy world interpretation.

5.5) *The flowers watered the girl.
5.6) *The girl was watered by the flowers.

Slobin called constructions like sentences 5.3) and 5.4) Irreversible actives and passives, respectively, in contrast to reversible actives and passives like sentences 5.1) and 5.2). Unlike his findings with ordinary reversible sentences, Slobin found no difference in evaluation time between irreversible active sentences and irreversible passive sentences. Subjects were able to judge the truth or falsity of irreversible actives and passives equally quickly.

From the point of view of the Derivational Theory of Complexity (see chapter four), this finding just did not make sense. Passive sentences have a more complicated transformational history than active sentences irrespective of their reversibility. Therefore, passive sentences should take longer to evaluate than active sentences even when those sentences are irreversible. However, Slobin's experimental finding could not be swept under the carpet. It clearly contradicted a fundamental prediction of the theory. Furthermore, the nature of the difference between reversible and irreversible sentences cannot be explained in terms of syntactic theory. Irreversible sentences are irreversible by virtue of their meaning and not because of any word-order rules. Slobin interpreted his results as indicating that **meaning** is a more important indicator of a sentence's complexity than its

transformational history. Furthermore, the notion that we detrans-
form sentences piecemeal in order to extract their deep structures
before proceeding to a meaningful analysis was contradicted by
Slobin's findings that irreversible passives did not take longer to
understand and evaluate than irreversible actives. Psycholinguists
were persuaded that the process of sentence understanding involves
the extraction of meaning from the very beginning of the comprehen-
sive process. There does not seem to exist an early stage of sentence
processing which is purely syntactic; meaning is involved from the
very start.

That meaning is involved in the process of sentence understanding has, of course, never been denied, even by the most syn-
tactically oriented psycholinguist. However, the relative difficulty of
formalising the meaning of a sentence into a system of rules made
transformational grammar seem an attractive tool for the study of
sentence understanding. As we saw in chapter four, it offers a mea-
surable, quantitative method of comparing sentence complexity. However, findings like those of Slobin's, quickly convinced psycholinguists that a more semantically oriented approach to the study of
language understanding was required. With hindsight, it is easy to
predict this rather obvious step in the progress of language research. However, the experimental hypotheses of psycholinguists in
the early sixties must be evaluated in the light of the methodological
and theoretical tools they had at their disposal. Transformational
grammar, during that period of psychological history, was simply the
best bet going.

5.7. Some Problems for a Transformational Description of Child Lan-
guage

Bloom's transformational approach to the description of two-word
utterances represented an important step forward in the study of child
language. However, we have seen that psycholinguists were becoming
dissatisfied with the Chomskyian paradigm. It was not long before
developmental psycholinguists followed suit. You will recall that the
grammar which Bloom wrote for Kathryn contained a transformational
component. One of the transformational rules, the reduction transformation, operated on deep structures that contained three terminal elements. The rule transformed the deep structure into a surface struc-

ture containing only two terminal elements. Bloom found it necessary to include the reduction transformation because the meaning relations expressed in Kathryn's utterances were more complicated than the two-word surface structures suggested. For example, Bloom noted the occurrence of three kinds of two-word constructions; agent-action (**mommy fix**); action-object (**hit ball**); agent-object (**mommy pumpkin**). Kathryn's mastery of these three constructions strongly suggest that she had knowledge of an underlying agent-action-object sentence pattern and that her two-word productions encoded just two elements of the underlying three element structure.

The fact that agent-object constructions occurred was especially striking since Kathryn would be unlikely to have heard them modelled in adult speech. On the other hand, the other two are relatively common in adult speech e.g. "Hit the ball". (action-object) or "The boy ran". (agent-action). We can neatly explain the occurrence of the agent-object construction in terms of the encoding of just two elements from an underlying three element structure. Thus, Bloom wrote her phrase structure rules so that they could generate three-element deep structures, corresponding to the agent-action-object sentence patterns. The reduction transformation did the job of deleting one of these elements to give the two-element surface structure. This deletion was necessary because of a psychological limit on sentence complexity which prevented Kathryn from combining three words.

Brown (1973) has criticised the use of the reduction transformation in Bloom's grammar for Kathryn. He points out that Bloom's data on the period of two-word utterances, contains examples of three-word combinations even during the early part of this period. Bloom did not include these utterances in the sample described by the grammar. Nevertheless, their occurrence shows that Kathryn was able to encode three-element constructions and so perhaps did not suffer the psychological limit on sentence complexity suggested by Bloom. This casts doubt on the necessity of including a reduction transformation in the grammar. Brown also points out that Kathryn continued to produce two-word utterances even when many of her utterances contained four or even five words i.e. when she undoubtedly did **not** suffer from a limit on sentence complexity. Two-word utterances may be motivated by reasons other than a reduction transformation. Brown argued that rather than complexity limiting the length of the child's utterances, the relevance of different aspects of the communicational situation is a more powerful constraint. In conversations with those around him, various aspects of the child's communication will be obvious to both speaker and listener as a result of mutual understanding and shared experience. The child, furthermore, expects his communication to be understood and so produces only the absolutely necessary components of the message. It is not until he ventures out in the world and needs to make his communications more explicit for less understanding individuals that he will start to encode the less necessary parts of the message.

Given that Bloom strongly advocated the use of meaning and context in the interpretation of children's utterances, it is surprising that she chose a grammatical solution, rather than a communicational solution, to the problem of the child's partial encoding of a supposed underlying sentence pattern. Furthermore, the reduction transformation introduced a type of complexity in the two-word period which later stages of language development did not possess. The child would need to unlearn the reduction transformation in the course of development if he was to achieve a stage of, say, three-word utterances. In this respect, a three-word stage would be a direct result of a simplification of the grammar of the two-word stage. In developmental psychology we are accustomed to development proceeding from the less complex to the more complex. The reduction transformation would represent a direct reversal of this trend.

Although Brown's criticism of the reduction transformation undermined the elegance of Bloom's transformational description, it by no means **proved** that Bloom was wrong. The reduction transformation might operate in the grammar despite Brown's arguments to the contrary. A more penetrating criticism concerned Bloom's method of describing children's two-word utterances in terms of abstract syntactic rules as opposed to a more semantically based approach. As we have seen, Bloom acknowledged the existence of a small set of meaning relations in children's two-word utterances and felt it important to include some account of these meaning relations in her grammar. However, she provided this account not by explicitly stating the relations in the grammar but by having the grammar generate distinguishable deep structures from which the different meaning relations could be interpreted. Thus we must **infer** from tables 5.6 and 5.7 that the two deep structures of "Mommy Sock" represent different meaning relations between "Mommy" and "Sock".

Like Chomsky, Bloom believed that it was necessary to have a level of sentence structure intermediate between the surface structure

of the sentence and its underlying semantic representation. This intermediate level, or deep structure, provided all the information necessary for a complete semantic interpretation of the sentence. It provided a means for describing such syntactic relations as subject and
object on which the different transformational rules could operate.
However, in such a grammar, it is necessary to have an additional
set of rules for constructing the semantic interpretation of the sentence. Why not instead have rules that map the semantic representation of the sentence directly onto its surface structure?

In the context of child language this argument seemed extremely
powerful. Many developmental psycholinguists were sceptical of the
rather sophisticated grammar that Bloom had written for Kathryn. It
suggested that the child knew an awful lot about her language e.g.
that words belonged to the category noun as opposed to verb or a
number of other grammatical categories? According to Bloom, Kathryn
also knew the structure of noun phrases and verb phrases and how
these relate to the sentence structure. In addition Kathryn possessed
a set of rules for interpreting and constructing the meanings embedded in her deep structures. Thus, Kathryn should be sensitive to
syntactic relations like subject and object since these provided the
primary means in the grammar of encoding and distinguishing semantic relations like agent-object or possessor-possessed. Unfortunately,
Bloom had no independent evidence that Kathryn had any knowledge of
such syntactic categories or relations. All Bloom had to go on was the
adequacy of her grammar in describing and predicting Kathryn's
two-word utterances. A grammar which could account equally well for
Kathryn's utterances yet not assume so much abstract knowledge would
quickly replace Bloom's transformational approach.

6   CASE GRAMMAR AND CHILD LANGUAGE.

6.1   Case Grammar

Towards the end of the sixties, a new movement began to emerge in the field of linguistics; a movement which attempted to describe sentences in terms of their meaning rather than their syntactic structures. This new approach was called **Case Grammar.** Historically, case grammar can be traced back to the study of languages which use inflections or cases rather than word-order to indicate the role of a word in a sentence. For example, languages like Latin, Finnish and Hungarian have a relatively free ordering of words in their sentences. Native speakers understand and signal distinctions like subject vs. object through a modification on the word itself. English, on the other hand, indicates the subject/object distinction through the use of word-order. However, that is not to say that English speakers do not use other means to signal a word's role in a sentence. For example, in sentence 6.1.), the preposition "with" is a reliable indicator that the noun it modifies "knife", is used as an

6.1.) John cut the rope with a knife.

instrument in the action identified by the verb "cut". In this case, the position of the word "knife" in the sentence is not a reliable indicator of its role as sentences 6.2.) and 6.3.) make clear.

6.2.) With a knife, John cut the rope.

6.3.) The rope was cut with a knife by John.

Clearly, any adequate account of language production and comprehension will need to explain the operation of both types of devices (word-order and inflections) in indicating the role of a word in a sentence.

6.4.) The boy kicked the ball.

	Deep Structure	Surface Structure
Subject	The boy	The boy
Object	the ball	the ball

6.5.) The ball was kicked by the boy.

	Deep Structure	Surface Structure
Subject	The boy	The ball
Object	the ball	the boy

In transformational grammar, the subject and object of a sentence are defined as those noun phrases in the sentence structure which are directly dominated by the sentence node and the verb phrase node respectively (see chapter four). It is also common to distinguish the deep structure subject and object of a sentence from its surface structure subject and object. For example, sentences 6.4.) and 6.5.) have different surface structure subjects and objects but their deep structure subjects and objects are identical.

In the case of the passive form, i.e. sentence 6.5.), the deep structure subject becomes the surface structure object whilst the deep structure object becomes the surface structure subject of the sentence. This reversal of roles is represented by the passive transformational rule of the grammar (see rule 4, chapter four p. 70). The passive transformation is thus defined in terms of its operation on the deep structure subject and object of the sentence. I have already argued that concepts like subject and object are not pure syntactic categories like noun phrase or verb phrase. The concepts, subject and object convey an element of meaning in the sense that they specify the relationship of the two noun phrases to the verb in the sentence. The passive transformation is sensitive to these two relationships and picks out for reversal just those two noun phrases which satisfy the necessary structural criteria for being a subject and an object. Although the concept subject specifies the relationship of a noun phrase to the verb, it does so only in a very general way. Consider sentences 6.6.)–6.8.).

6.6.) John cut the rope.
6.7.) The rope was cut by John.
6.8.) The knife cut the rope.

Each sentence has a different subject, i.e. John, the rope and the knife respectively. And each subject has a different relationship to the verb. That is, John is the person who does the cutting, the rope is the object that is cut whilst the knife is the instrument used to do the cutting. Clearly, the concept subject does not give a precise specification of the relationship between a given noun phrase and the verb of the sentence. Transformational grammar goes some way to overcoming this difficulty by classifying "John" as the deep structure subject of sentence 6.7.) and so maintaining the same relationship to the verb as "John" in sentence 6.6.). However, transformational grammar cannot solve this problem in sentence 6.8.). "The knife" is the deep structure subject of the sentence and so has the same syntactic relation to the verb as "John" in sentences 6.6.) and 6.7.).

In 1968, Fillmore argued that a grammar should be able to specify the relationships that hold between the noun phrases and the verb in a sentence, more accurately than the vague syntactic relations of "subject" and "object". He proposed that these relationships are specified at a deeper level of sentence structure than Chomsky's syntactic deep structure. This deeper level gives a more specific representation of the sentence's meaning. At the heart of Fillmore's theory is a categorisation system for assigning the noun phrases in a sentence to certain meaningful roles of cases. Fillmore presumed that these case categories represented a universal set of innate concepts which are expressed in all languages. Table 6.1. outlines the case system he used.

Fillmore's Case Concepts

Case Name	Definition	Example (designated case is in bold type)
Agentive A	The typically animate perceived instigator of action.	**John** opened the door. The door was opened by **John.**
Instrumental (I)	The inanimate force or object causally involved in the state or action named by the verb.	The **key** opened the door. John opened the door with the **key.**
Dative (D)	The animate being affected by the state or action named by the verb.	**Adam** sees Eve. John murdered **Bill** John gave the book to **Bill. Daddy** has a study.
Factitive (F)	The object or being resulting from the state or action named by the verb.	God created **woman.** John built a **table.**
Locative (L)	The location or spatial orientation of the state or action named by the verb.	The sweater is on the **chair. Chicago** is windy. John walked to **school**
Objective (O)	The semantically most neutral case: Anything representable by a noun whose role in the state or action named by the verb depends on the meaning of the verb itself.	Adam sees **Eve.** The **sweater** is on the chair. John opened the **door.**

Source: Fillmore 1968

Table 6.1.

The first thing to notice about Table 6.1. is that the different case relations do not have a one-to-one mapping onto either surface structure elements or Chomskyian deep structure elements. The different cases can all play the role of sentence subject and individual cases can play different roles in the syntactic structure of the sentence. For example, in the instrumental case (I), "The key" can play the role of sentence subject or alternatively, object of the preposition "with". Fillmore provides a set of rules for generating sentences with the grammar. These rules are not intended to give a complete description of case grammar. Rather they give us a flavour of its general outline. A summary of these rules are given in table 6.2.

A Case Grammar

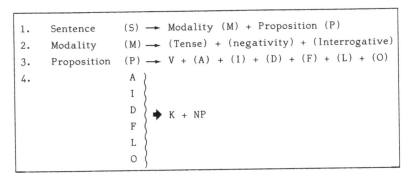

Table 6.2.

The immediate constituents of a sentence are not noun phrase and verb phrase, but modality and proposition. Modality includes information about the tense of the verb, whether the proposition is to be negated and the function of the sentence i.e. whether it is to be used to make a statement, give a command, or ask a question, etc. Fillmore does not develop this constituent in his 1968 paper, but concentrates on the proposition of the sentence. Rule 3 indicates that a proposition consists of a verb (V) plus a list of case relations. The letters are defined by the appropriate cases in Table 6.1. The parentheses indicate that not all cases are necessarily included in the proposition. In fact, Fillmore argues that the verb provides a framework for the different cases that are included in the proposition. Consider sentences 6.9.) – 6.12.).

6.9.) The door opened.
6.10.) John opened the door.
6.11.) The wind opened the door.
6.12.) John opened the door with a chisel.

These sentences suggest that the only case which is always included in the proposition together with the verb "open" is the Objective case (O) represented by the noun phrase "the door". All the other cases, e.g. John (A), chisel (I) are optional. The verb "cut" (see sentences 6.6.)-6.8.)) would also seem to set the same constraints on the selection of different case relations. On the other hand, the verb "put" requires born the objective and locative case to be specified, whilst the agentive case is optional.

We can thus see how we might classify verbs according to their case frames i.e. in terms of those cases which are obligatory and those which are optional. Fillmore suggests that these case frames are part of our linguistic knowledge about verbs. This knowledge specifies the potential relation of different noun phrases to the verb in a sentence and also sets constraints on the type of noun phrases that can play the role of certain cases. For example, the agent and dative cases require an animate noun phrase whilst the locative case needs a noun phrase with a spatial component. The noun "idea" could not play the role of the locative case since it has no spatial component.

The propositional structure of case grammar gives us an understanding of the meaning relations underlying the sentences of a language. However, the propositional structure does not in itself explain how we get to the surface structure of the sentence. We still need to be able to explain that in sentences like "The boy hits the girl", we know that it is the boy who is doing the hitting and not the girl. Different languages solve this problem in different ways. For example, many languages, like Latin, Greek, Finnish and Russian which have relatively free word-order inflect the noun phrases in a sentence (rather like English inflects verbs for number agreement) in order to indicate case relationships like agent, instrument, dative, etc. Languages like English tend to use word-order rules to indicate the word's role in the sentence. However, word-order rules give rise to relations like subject and object which are not specific enough to indicate the case which a particular noun phrase is fulfilling. How then do we use word-order rules to uncover the propositional structure of the sentence?

This problem is one of the main difficulties facing case grammar and here we can only provide a glimpse of the still sought after solution. Fillmore's general solution to this problem is represented in rule 4 of table 6.2. That is, cases are realised in the surface structure of a sentence as a noun phrase plus a case marker. The case marker associated with the noun phrase indicates the case role of the noun phrase in relation to the verb, e.g. agent or instrument. In many languages, as we have already seen, case markers are realised as inflections on the noun phrase. In English, we often use prepositions to indicate the case of the noun phrase. In other words, the case marker K is generally realised as a preposition in English. Fillmore has outlined a set of rules which specifies how prepositions operate to indicate case in English. These are given in table 6.3. It is worth noting how the marker for the instrument case changes from "by" to "with" when the agent case is included in the prepositional structure. Furthermore, the prepositional marker for the locative case is the only marker which conveys any semantic content.

The Role of Prepositions in Case Grammar

Case	Preposition	Example
A	by	The door was opened **by John.**
I (if there is no A)	by	The case was hit **by a stone.**
I (If there is an A)	with	John hit the car **with a stone.**
O + F	typically no preposition	John opened **the door.** John built **a table.**
D	to	He gave the present **to Mary.**
L	in, on, over, under, etc.	The car is **in the garage.** The dog sits **under the table.**

Source: Fillmore, 1968.

Table 6.3.

Prepositions represent one of the devices which English uses to indicate the relationship of a noun phrase to a verb. However, not all noun phrases in English sentences are associated with prepositional case markers. A swift perusal of the examples in table 6.3. will reveal that a majority of the noun phrases have no prepositional markers at all. How then do we identify the case role of these unmarked noun phrases in the sentence? The majority of unmarked noun phrases are those represented by the syntactic relations subject and object. Fillmore has proposed a rule which assigns case roles to the syntactic subject of the sentence in accordance with presence of other case relations in the propositional structure. Our knowledge of the rule enables us to signal or identify the case role that the subject plays in the sentence. The most general rule for the assignment of cases to the subject is as follows:

> **Rule 5.** If there is an A, it becomes the subject; if there is an I, it becomes the subject, otherwise the subject is the O.

We can see this process at work in sentences 6.13.) − 6.16).

> 6.13.) The window broke.
> 6.14.) John broke the window.
> 6.15.) A hammer broke the window.
> 6.16.) John broke the window with a hammer.

In 6.13.), the objective case "the window" becomes the subject because there are no other cases present. In 6.15.), which lacks an agent, the instrument "hammer" takes precedence over the objective "window" as subject whereas in 6.16.) the agent "John" takes precedence as subject over both the objective and instrumental cases[3]. When assigning the subjects of sentences 6.14.) and 6.15.) to their various case roles, we use our knowledge that a noun phrase acting as an agent must have the property of being animate. Therefore, the subject of 6.15.), "a hammer", cannot be assigned to the agent role. Furthermore, our knowledge that the case frame of the verb "break" takes an obligatory O case with the A and I cases optional, enables us to decipher via rule 5, the case roles of the subjects of sentences 6.13.) and 6.15.). In sentence 6.16.), the preposition "with" identifies the case role of "a hammer" and the other case roles are assigned in accordance with rule 5).

---

[3] Note that the passive form of 6.15.) − "The window was broken by the hammer." − does **not** change the deep structure subject from "window" to "hammer". The subject remains "hammer". When referring to the subject of a sentence it is understood that the deep structure subject is implied.

There would also seem to be a rule for assigning case roles to the object of a sentence. Fillmore does not provide us with such a rule but sentences 6.13.) - 6.16.) suggest that the objective case takes precedence so long as it does not act as the subject of the sentence. In such cases, e.g. 6.13.), the sentence is objectless. Note that this does not mean that the verb's objective case slot is empty. In 6.13.) the subject of the sentence plays the objective case role. The concept "object of sentence" should not be confused with the case role "objective".

Fillmore also states that only one representative of a given case relationship may appear in the same proposition. This constraint, together with the requirement that an agent be represented by an animate noun phrase, accounts for the unacceptability of sentences like:

6.17.) *A hammer broke the glass with a chisel.
6.18.) *The car broke the window with a fender.

When a noun phrase acts as subject or object, its prepositional case marker is deleted from the sentence and we use knowledge like rule 5) and the verb's case frame to assign the noun phrase to a particular case role. However, these constraints are not always adequate to specify the case role taken by a noun phrase acting as a subject or object. For example, consider the two verbs "give" and "receive". The two verbs are essentially synonymous in that the two sentences;

6.19.) John gave a present to Mary.
6.20.) Mary received a present from John.

represent the same underlying event. In fact, "give" and "receive" have identical case frames in that any subset of the case roles A, I and D can be taken by the verbs. However, the verbs differ in that "give" assigns the agent case to subject position when that case occurs in the underlying proposition P, just as rule 5 would predict (see 6.19.), whilst "receive" over-rides rule 5 and assigns the dative case "Mary" to subject even though the agent case may be present in the proposition (see 6.20.)[4]. Clearly, knowledge of these spe-

---

[4] Also note that "receive" also implements the operation of an irregular preposition "from" to indicate the agent role. "From"

cial assignment rules is necessary in deciphering the case relations of noun phrases in sentences which contain verbs like "receive".

The description of a semantically based grammar like case grammar is not an easy task. In fact, we have only skimmed the surface of the quagmire of problems that case grammar has to solve in order to become an adequate grammar of English. However, case grammar is not alone in this respect. A transformational grammar has yet to be written that can adequately describe the English language. That case grammar tries to capture both meaning structures and syntactic structures simultaneously does not make its task any easier. It is also important to realise that case grammar does not discard syntactic notions completely. Indeed, it would be foolhardy to do so. Word-order rules that define syntactic relations like subject and object are clearly part of the native speaker's linguistic knowledge. As we have seen (see p. 106), such syntactic relations help us to account for our ability to construct passive forms. Fillmore recognises the importance of the relations subject and object in terms of their capacity to signal a variety of case roles. The rules for assigning particular case roles to subject and object are just another version of the case marker which may otherwise be realised as a preposition or an inflection on the noun phrase. The advantage of case grammar is that it takes us beyond a purely abstract description of sentence structure at the deep syntactic level to a formal system for representing sentence meaning. For the psycholinguist who was finding that **meaning** was an important determinant of sentence complexity, rather than transformational history, Fillmore's case grammar was a welcome sight.

6.2 Case Grammar in Child Language.

It was not long before students of child language began to feel that case grammar might provide a more psychologically valid description of children's two-word utterances. To begin with, the constituent cases of Fillmore's grammar (see table 6.1.) represented concepts with which the young child might be familiar. Cases like agentive,

---

would normally be used to indicate a locative case as in "He came from town". The use of "from" in this context undoubtedly reflects the directional property of receiving. From the point of view of the receiver, an object comes "from" the giver whilst the giver gives "to".

instrumental and objective all seemed to be part of the meanings conveyed by the child's two-word utterances. Furthermore, a case grammar approach to children's language would by-pass the need to postulate an intervening level of deep structure between the surface structure of the utterance and its underlying semantic representation.

At first glance, case grammar would seem an inappropriate system for describing two-word utterances. According to Fillmore, the case role of a noun phrase in an utterance is indicated by a case marker. In English, case markers are generally realised as prepositions in the surface structure of the utterance. Children's two-word utterances are almost completely lacking in prepositions, as they are in inflections which other languages use to mark case roles. Two-word utterances are also characteristically lacking in tense, mood, number agreement, etc., all aspects of sentence constructions generally associated with the modality component of Fillmore's case grammar. However, the possibility exists that children's two-word utterances reflect a knowledge of the underlying propositional structure in case grammar. The propositional structure consisted of a verb plus its associated cases (obligatory and optional). Two-word utterances might be an encoding of components in this underlying structure.

The application of this hypothesis has some intuitively appealing results. Consider the case frame associated with the verb "open". We saw earlier that "open" takes one obligatory case role (the objective) and two optional cases (agentive and instrumental). We might represent this case frame as in;

$$\text{"open"} = V + O + (A) + (I)$$

where the identity sign indicates that "open" is a verb and the parentheses signal that the enclosed cases are optional. Now suppose that a young child knows the case frame for the verb "open", as well as the names of objects which can play the role of various cases associated with "open". This would entail the child knowing, for example, what type of objects can be used as instruments and what type of objects can act as agents. If the child then produces the two-word utterance "Door open" we would be justified in assuming that the utterance represented an encoding of the propositional component of the grammar; namely, the verb and its associated objective case. Furthermore, we could specify the meaning relation between the two words in the utterance by reference to the case frame of the verb, i.e. "Door open" is an action-object relation. Other utterances like "John open" or "John door" could similarly be assigned agent-action and agent-object relations respectively, by reference to the case frame of "open".

Case grammar thus seems to provide a tool for describing the meaning relations in children's two-word utterances that does not require the postulation of an intermediate level of deep structure. What case grammar does require is an understanding of the various case roles that are associated with verbs. Fillmore had already suggested that these case roles are universal and innate. Thus the early stages of language development seem to reduce to a process of discovering the case configurations associated with different verbs. Two-word utterances represented a stage in the development of the full expression of a sentence's underlying propositional structure.

6.3 Meaning Relations

If Fillmore is correct in his claim that the case roles named in table 6.1. are universal and presumably innate, then we have a basis for predicting what kind of meaning relations the child might encode in his two-word utterances. We have just seen how relations like agent-action, action-object and agent-object can emerge from a knowledge of the case frame of the verb "open". What other relations might occur? According to case grammar, case relations are built around the verb. If we assume that the child's knowledge of verb case frames is sufficiently complex that all possible combinations of cases are realisable, then a total of 21 different meaning relations may be produced by the child, i.e. all the possible combinations of the six case frames and the verb itself. This calculation is based on the assumption that there are no restrictions on the meaning relations the child produces other than the case roles specified in the grammar. We also assume that the child has a sufficiently rich knowledge of verb case frames and the conditions which objects must fulfil to play the role of the various cases, e.g. the agent and dative cases can only be represented by animate objects.

In fact, we find that the range of meaning relations expressed in two-word utterances is much more limited. Brown (1973) reports that only 8 relations are common for all children in the corpus of data he has analysed. This data is based on the two-word utterances

116

of 10 children from 5 different language communities (American English, Swedish, Mexican Spanish, Finnish and Samoan). These are given in table 6.4. together with some examples. You will notice that Brown does not express the relations in terms identical with those described in Fillmore's case grammar. For example, relation 6 (possessor-possessed) is not obtained from case grammar at all but is an alternative classification of a meaning relation in child language. In case grammar terms, the possessor-possessed relation would be analysed as dative-objective on the grounds that in adult language, the genitive construction "Adam's ball" is derived from the proposition "Adam has a ball". "Adam" plays the role of the animate being affected by the state named by the verb "has", i.e. the dative case. "Ball" plays the semantically neutral case of the objective.

Meaning Relations in Two-Word Utterances

	Relation	Example
1.	Agent-Action	Mommy Fix.
2.	Action-Object	Hit ball.
3.	Agent-Object	Mommy pumpkin. (is cutting up)
4.	Action-Location	Put floor.
5.	Entity-Location	Baby table. (is eating at a)
6.	Possessor-Possessed	Adam ball.
7.	Attribute-Entity	Big dog.
8.	Demon-Entity	This house.

Source: Brown, 1973.

Table 6.4.

It is important to realise in this connection that Fillmore's case grammar was written to describe adult language. The classificatory system for the meaning relations expressed in children's language may not map directly on to those used by adults and consequently alternative descriptive systems may be required. Certainly, the description possessor-possessed seems to capture better the relation holding between "Adam" and "ball" than does dative-objective. More importantly, the relation dative-objective encompasses a greater variety of meaning relations than does the relation possessor-possessed. The relationship between Adam and Eve in "Adam sees Eve" is also assigned a dative-objective analysis in Fillmore's case grammar (see table 6.1.). Yet we would wish to distinguish this relationship from that of possessor-possessed.

When we take into account Brown's reclassification, we find that only 7 of the possible 21 combinations occur in children's two-word utterances. The attribute-entity relation is, in fact, classified by Fillmore's grammar under the same combination as relation 2 in Brown's system. For reasons which we need not consider here, adjectives are treated as verbs in case grammar descriptions. Thus attribute-entity is a special case of the verb-objective combination. Surprisingly, demonstrative-entity cannot be easily classified within the case grammar system and so appears as an additional relation in Brown's classification. Finally, entity-location (relation 5) confounds two combinations that case grammar would distinguish; namely, agent-location and object-location. Thus, Brown's 8 relations consist of seven combinations which can be distinguished in terms of case grammar plus an additional relation (Demonstrative-Entity) which case grammar does not classify.

All this re-classifying and cross-classifying indicates a fundamental problem in the study of the meaning relations in children's two-word utterances. It is difficult to be certain that our interpretation of children's meanings is correct. Different classification systems represent different views as to which are the important distinctions encoded by children in their utterances. Thus, Brown distinguishes between Action-Object and Attribute-Entity while Fillmore confounds the two. In the final analysis, we must search for a classification system that can describe and predict children's utterances in a fashion that is consistent with what the child knows. For example, if a child failed to show any understanding of the concept of location it would be foolish to describe his utterances in terms of a relation which utilised this case role.

The development of a classification system for describing meaning relations is much like the process of trying to write a grammar for the word-order rules in children's language. One keeps developing new descriptions until one seems to find an adequate fit. The advantage of describing children's language in terms of meaning relations is that we cannot only use what he says to ascertain the goodness-of-fit but also what he seems to know about the world, as a justification for attributing particular types of linguistic knowledge. It is precisely this latter type of evidence that Bloom was lacking in her study.

It is clear that our admittedly crude adaptation of Fillmore's case grammar for predicting the number of meaning relations produced by the young child, does not match up to the child's reality. Generally, young children only produce seven of 21 meaning relations that can be derived from Fillmore's case grammar. The question arises as to the cause of this limitation. You will remember that Fillmore claimed that each of his six case roles could be identified in all languages yet studied by linguists and so were presumably innate. It was because of their innate character that we assumed that children would know all six case roles and so combine them in all possible ways depending, of course, on what meanings they wished-ed to express. The children's failure to produce all 21 meaning relations may result from their not knowing some of the case roles proposed by Fillmore.

An analysis of the meaning relations described in Table 6.4. reveals that two of the case roles are missing from the children's two-word utterances. None of the relations encode the Instrumental or the Factitive cases. That is, the children seem to have mastered only four of Fillmore's case roles; Agentive, Objective, Locative and Dative. If we remove the Instrumental and Factitive cases, the number of potential combinations reduces dramatically from 21 to 10; a number much closer to the observed 7 relations. Thus, Fillmore's assumption that his six case roles are innate appears questionable. At least, children at the two-word stage of language development do not appear to be in command of the Instrumental and Factitive cases. If the case roles are innate, a reason is needed to explain why these two latter cases emerge later in the child's language than the other four cases.

By questioning the innateness assumption, we have reduced the number of possible case combinations to 10. Yet we only observe 7 relations. We know that the child has mastered four case roles. We must therefore look to some other source to explain the discrepancy. In calculating the number of possible meaning relations that the child might produce, it was also assumed that the child possesses a sufficiently rich repertoire of verbs such that all possible case frames are represented. If two cases are not part of a case frame associated with a verb, the child would have no grounds for encoding those cases in the same utterance. For example, consider the agentive-dative case combination. One way that this particular combination might be manifested is through the case frame associated with the verb "give". As sentence 6.21.) indicates "give" takes the agentive, the objective and the dative cases.

> 6.21.) John gave the present to Mary.
> (Agentive)   (Objective) (Dative).

Thus, in the context of one person giving a present to another, the two-word utterance "John Mary" might be said to encode the meaning relation agentive-dative. However, suppose the child did not possess the verb "give" and its associated case frame, or for that matter, any other verb that associated the agentive and dative cases, in his vocabulary. There would be no underlying propositional structure (generated from the case frame) from which to construct the case relation agentive-dative. The child would lack a sufficiently differentiated system of case frames.

It would appear that this explanation can account for the missing 3 meaning relations. Although the child has four cases represented in his vocabulary, only three of them are found in combination with the verb and each other. These are the agentive, objective and locative cases. The fourth case, the dative, only occurs in combination with the objective case to produce the meaning relation dative-objective which is the case grammar description of the possessor-possessed relation. The child fails to produce any of the other meaning relations in which the dative can play a part; namely, agent-dative, action-dative, and locative-dative. Thus, we can identify the three missing meaning relations by arguing that the child's verb case frames are insufficiently differentiated with respect to dative case. The meaning relations that do occur are those which can be generated through the combination of the verb (action) and the three cases, agentive, objective, and locative. The number of possible relational combinations with four elements is just 6. The single occurrence of the dative case in the dative-objective relation yields the total of seven meaning relations identified by Brown and classifiable in case grammar terms.

The adaption of Fillmore's case grammar to the description of child language has enabled us to by-pass the need of attributing linguistic deep structures to children in the two-word stage of language development. We have seen how the meaning relations encoded in two-word utterances can be captured by a semantic representation which maps directly onto the surface structure of the utterances. This semantic representation is described in terms of a propositional structure built out of verb case frames which the child has mastered. However, we have also found it necessary to limit the number of case roles that we attribute to the child thus questioning Fillmore's claim that case roles are innate. Furthermore, the evidence seems to suggest that the child does not command the variety of case frame constellations that his knowledge of individual cases might permit. In particular, the dative case fails to achieve its full combinatorial potential. We have attributed this to a lack of verbs in the child's vocabulary which take the dative case. In this way, we have managed to limit the number of meaning relations representable in the propositional structure to 7.

However, a quick perusal of the verbs present in children's two-word utterances will reveal that they include a selection which does indeed take the dative case. For example, in Table 6.4. the verbs "fix" and "hit" can take the dative as in 6.22.) and 6.23) respectively:

6.22.) Mommy fixed the toy **for Adam.**
6.23.) Mary hit the ball **to Daddy.**

From an adult perspective, the verbs used by young children should enable them to produce the missing dative relations. The argument that children lack verbs taking the dative case and so cannot produce the three missing dative relations appears to be misleading. However, just because the verbs "hit" and "fix" take the dative in the adult grammar does not mean that they are similarly defined by children. Although the verbs may have the same fundamental meaning for both adult and child, it is possible that the child has not yet discovered all the different situations in which the action described by the verb is used. In case grammar terms, the child may only partially know the meaning of the verb "hit", e.g. he may know the action described by the verb and that the verb takes the agentive and objective cases. The child may not yet know that the dative case is part of the case frame for the verb "hit". If he does not know that the dative is part of a verb's case frame, the child will be unable to encode meaning relations containing the dative from the proposition created by that verb's case frame. In other words, we can explain the missing three dative relations by arguing that a child's verb case frames are generally lacking the dative case, even though the equivalent adult verb case frames may contain the dative.

The development of meaning relations in children's language can be seen as a process of learning which cases go with which verbs as well as discovering the verbs and the cases themselves. Of course, it is undoubtedly the case that the sorting out and discovery processes go hand-in-hand. For example, the child surely comes to learn verbs as he learns the different cases associated with them. But the evidence presented here strongly suggests that the association of cases with their relevant verbs is not immediate. The child may learn that some cases, like the dative, go with some verbs before he learns that they can be associated with other verbs. In this way, the propositional structures underlying children's utterances come to encode more and more aspects of reality. This in turn, permits an increasing range of meaning relations to be expressed by the child.

6.4   Word-Order and Propositional Structure

In our review of the case grammar approach to children's language, we have hypothesised that the child's two-word utterances are a surface manifestation of a much richer underlying propositional structure. In this respect, our argument duplicates that of Bloom's in her description of Kathryn's two-word utterances. However, the case grammar approach differs from Bloom's transformational approach in that it does not postulate a level of deep structure. The advantage of the case grammar approach is that it provides a rational framework for describing the meaning relations in children's utterances without having to attribute the child with abstract syntactic knowledge like subject or object. Nevertheless, what evidence is there that the child really does have in mind a rich propositional structure when he produces a two-word utterance?

So far the evidence we have presented, though consistent with a propositional hypothesis, is by no means conclusive. The child might produce utterances with similar meaning relations to those described above yet without recourse to a linguistic propositional structure. For example, he may conceptualise ongoing situations in terms of elements like agent, action, object and location and simply encode various elements of his conceptual analysis in terms of words appropriate to the elements in that context. We do not need to postulate that the child collects all these elements together in the form of the linguistic structure we call a proposition. The meaning relations in children's language might be explained without a semantic level of representation (i.e. the proposition) just as they can be explained without a level of deep structure. Indeed, the lack of prepositions (the traditional markers of case in English) in children's early language suggests that a conceptually based approach might be a more appropriate perspective than case grammar.

However, you will remember from our discussion of case grammar that prepositions were not the only device for signalling case role in English. Word-order is a fairly reliable, though complicated, device for signalling the role of a noun phrase in a sentence. If we could find evidence that the child is using a device for indicating case role then we would be more justified in assuming that a child's two-word utterances reflected a richer, underlying propositional structure. The existence of such a device would, in turn, indicate the existence of a representational structure upon which the device operated. It would be pointless having a device that did not operate on anything.

Brown (1973) has claimed that such a device exists, at least for American-English children in the two-word stage of language development. He has found that children use word-order to indicate the case role of the word in the utterance. In fact, the word-order device operates in a similar way to the rule for assigning case roles to the subject relation in adult language described in rule 5 (p. 112). Brown observed that he could predict the position of a word in a two-word utterance according to its case role in the underlying propositional structure. For example, if a word is assigned the role of agent and the agent case is encoded in the utterance then that word will always take the initial position. On the other hand, a word representing the objective case can occur in either position in the utterance, initial or final, depending upon which other case is encoded. In fact, Brown found that if he restricted the propositional structures to verbs (actions), agentives, objectives and locatives (the prevalent cases in two-word utterances) then he could predict the ordering of words according to the following schema:

Word-Order Schema

> **Agent – Action – Object – Location**

Thus if words corresponding to the verb (action) and the objective case are chosen for encoding in the two-word utterance then the objective word will occur in the final position. If words corresponding to the objective and locative cases are encoded then the objective word will occur in the initial position. Locatives always come last. You might care to check Table 6.4. to confirm this schema on the limited data available. Brown found no exceptions for any of his English- speaking subjects.

In harmony with case grammar and his criticism of Bloom's reduction transformation, Brown suggested that the existence of a word-order device for indicating case roles in two-word utterances provides some support for the view that a rich propositional structure underlies the child's early utterances. This propositional entity may be considered a distinct level of representation from a purely conceptual analysis in that it gathers together the elements of conceptual analysis into a single structure on which the device can act. That the elements are collected together into a single propositional entity is indicated by the fact that case roles like the objective and the verb are sensitive to the other case roles for their positioning in the utterance. We would not expect this ordering effect if the child was simply encoding the elements of a conceptual analysis as they occurred to him. Even though some case roles may be more **salient** for the child than others, and so are encoded first, it is unlikely that it is always say the agent which the child is most interested in. Indeed, a good number of utterances do not even encode the agent case. Brown argues that the child chooses which elements of the propositional structure to encode on the basis of what he expects his listener to understand implicitly. Thus some elements will not be encoded because the child expects the listener to know them already from the ongoing context. The utterance puts the "meat" on this supposed shared understanding and in such a way that the words are ordered to conform with the schema outlined above. Thus, although **salience** might be used to explain **what** the child says, it does not explain **how** he actually says what he says. We appear to need a level of propositional structure intervening between the surface structure of the utterance and the child's conceptual understanding, if we are to understand the actual form of his utterances.

The findings of pivot grammar (see p. 85-87) would also seem to fit into this propositional approach to children's language. You will recall that pivot grammar identified three grammatical categories into which children's words in the two-word stage could be classified. Open words could occur in any position in the utterance as well as alone. Pivot words were supposed to occur only in the initial or final position, never alone and only in combination with open class words. Now consider the categories agent and location in the word-order schema defined above. We have seen that when the agent is encoded in the utterance, it always takes the initial position whereas the locative always takes the final position. Thus words which tend to play the role of agent or locative will also tend to occur in the initial or final position of the utterance respectively. In this way, the word-order device for indicating case roles in two-word utterances will contribute to the pivot-like nature of such utterances. Indeed, if we look at the analysis of Andrew's utterances offered by Braine (see p. 87), we see that at least one of the initial pivots "I" could justifiably be reclassified as an agent. Of the final pivots, "off" and "in there" would seem to have clear location qualities and "by" might also be similarly reclassified (though with less certainty). The pivot character of two-word utterances can be seen as an outcome of their underlying propositional structure and the rules for ordering the constituent cases of the proposition in the surface utterances.

However, it is important to note that the propositional approach is more flexible in its word-order rules than pivot grammar. Whereas pivot grammar specified that particular words must occur in particular positions, the word-order device for indicating case roles specifies only that certain cases must occur in particular positions; namely, agentive and locative. Since individual words can play the role of different cases in a propositional structure, they are able to occur in different positions in the utterances even though agentive and locative cannot. On the other hand, if some words are frequently (if not always) associated with the agentive case e.g. "I" or the locative case e.g. "off", "in there" and "by" then they too will occur in fixed positions. It is no surprise that we can account for a greater proposition of the final pivot words than initial pivots with this explanation. Words representing animate beings who can play the role of agent, e.g. proper names, are nearly always also used in the objective and dative case roles. Location words like "off" and "in there" are less able to switch cases and are often stuck in the locative. Thus words which can play the agentive case role need not necessarily do so and need not have an initial pivot character[5]. Location words cannot change case roles easily and so will have a final-pivot character. This new approach to describing the meaning relations in children's two-word utterances can, therefore, also be used to describe some word-order regularities in those utterances in a more powerful, yet more flexible manner than previous attempts.

The existence of a word-order device for indicating case roles in two-word utterances is good evidence for the existence of a rich underlying propositional structure. However, Brown's evidence for such a device is by no means conclusive. The gap in the argument concerns the centrality of the verb in case grammar descriptions. We have discussed how the propositional structure underlying a two-word utterance is constructed from a verb plus its associated case frame. The case frame may not be so differentiated as the equivalent adult form but the principle of propositional representation is the same; the verb plus its associated cases. The verb, then plays a central role in determining the structure of the underlying proposition. Indeed, we can only attribute the underlying propositional structure "Agent-Action-Object-Location" to a particular two-word utterance, if the verb concerned takes the case roles agentive, objective and locative like "put" and "hit" as in sentences 6.24.) and 6.25.).

6.24.) John put the car in the garage.
6.25.) John hit Bill in the face.

But how can we know that the verb, as used by the child, takes the cases specified by the grammar? We cannot rely on the adult's definition of the case frame since the child's configuration may well

---

5 "I" is the special case where a word can only occur in a particular case role, i.e. the agentive.

be different. The only evidence available is the verb's combination with case roles in the two-word utterances themselves. For example, consider how we might infer that the child's use of the verb "put" involves the same case frame as implied by sentence 6.24.). To be confident that the child knew that the verb "put" took the agentive, objective and locative case roles we would expect to find "put" combined with each of these case roles in the corpus of the child's speech, as in 6.26.)-6.28.).

    6.26.) John put.
    6.27.) Put car.
    6.28.) Put garage.

The child's utterance of these three combinations would be strong evidence for a knowledge of the case frame of "put" as well as a word-order device for indicating case roles. On the other hand, the occurrence of utterances like 6.29.)-6.31.), though consistent with such

    6.29.) John car.
    6.30.) John garage.
    6.31.) Car garage.

an analysis, is not direct evidence for the child's knowledge of the case frame of "put" itself, and consequently inadequate evidence for the existence of an adult-like propositional structure underlying such utterances.

Although Brown was able to predict the position of a word in a two-word utterance according to its case role in the hypothesised, underlying propositional structure, ˙ he had no independent evidence for the existence of the propositional structure itself, i.e. utterances of the form 6.26.)-6.28.) which provide firm foundations for inferring that the child has mastered a differentiated verb case frame. Instead, Brown inferred the existence of an underlying propositional structure on the basis of such utterances as "Put car", "John car" and "car garage". Such a set of utterances might provide evidence for word-order rules in the child's speech and even evidence that the child has associated the objective case role with the verb "put". However, they do not indicate that the child has yet associated the agentive and locative cases with the verb "put". And since propositional structures are constructed from the verb's case frame, such utterances fail to provide convincing evidence for the existence of a rich, underlying propositional structure. The two-word utterance "John car" might well reflect the meaning relation "Agent-Object". But if we have no evidence that the child has associated the agentive and objective case with the verb "put" we cannot reasonably claim that the meaning relation underlying "John car" is mediated by the verb in a propositional structure. Only the co-occurrence of utterances like 6.26.)-6.28.) would justify this interpretation. So long as we lack the kind of evidence that could justify our attributing differentiated case frames to verbs in early child language, we cannot with any confidence conclude that a linguistic propositional structure underlies two-word, or three- or four-word utterances for that matter.

7   ORIGINS OF SYNTAX

7.1   Traditional Approaches

In the previous chapter we found that there is insufficient evidence to conclude that the child has mastered propositional structures at the two-word stage of language development. However, so long as we accept the analysis of the component words of two-word utterances into categories like, agent, action, object and location, we need to take account of Brown's finding that he could predict the position of a word in the utterance according to its meaning relation with the other word. In other words, how does the child learn to order the words in his utterances so that they conform to the rules embodied in the schema "Agent-Action-Object-Location"? (see p. 124).

   An obvious answer to this question is that the child copies or imitates the utterances that he hears around him. That is to say, he uses the language of his parents and other adults as a model for his own language. The child notices the word-order regularities of adult-speech and incorporates it into his own language. For example, the typical, or canonical, form of English sentences follows the structure Subject-Verb-Object which when translated into semantic terms typically gives the structure Agent-Action-Object. This structure preserves the order of the first three elements of the four element schema which Brown described for the basis of word-order in two-word utterances. Indeed, Brown's schema would itself seem to observe the typical, or canonical form in English for the four elements involved. (For example, see sentence 6.24.). The child could learn to order his words in the way he does by observing how adults typically order the words in their own speech.

Preliminary Approaches to Language Development

At one level of analysis, this explanation of how children learn the syntax of their language must be correct. Different languages order their words in different ways. Therefore, the only way that the child could discover the appropriate order for his language is to listen to the language used by his parents and other adults around him. However, the argument is inadequate for a number of reasons. We have discussed some of them in the context of Chomsky's Universal Grammar. For example, syntactic structures are too complicated to learn through a process of listening and subsequent deduction of rules. And adults do not always speak in well-formed grammatical sentences. However, in the context of case grammar additional difficulties emerge. For example, we have seen how the subject of a sentence does not need to be an agent as in "Mary received a present from John" or "The chopper cut down the tree". Datives and Instruments can also act as sentence subjects. The problem is that adults do not always use the canonical sentence structure Agent-Action-Object. Consequently, if children were imitating the adult model we would expect to see a wider variety of word-orders in their two-word utterances. Agents would not necessarily come first and locatives last. Paradoxically, we find children learning a set of word-order rules that cannot be found in the adult language. However, if adults used only the canonical sentence form in their speech to children then the paradox could be resolved. Adults would then be presenting children with a model that fitted Brown's schema perfectly.

Another problem for the imitation model of syntax acquisition is that it provides no explanation of how children identify the components of the structure, i.e. Agent, Action, Object and Location. If the model is to be non-trivial, it must assume that children are able to generalise particular instances of adult uses of the agent category (e.g. "John" or "I") to other uses of their own. In other words, the children would need to know which words can play the role of agent, action, object or location. Furthermore, the child would need to have some means for deciding that the first word in the adult utterance was, indeed, an agent whilst the final word represented, say, the object role. The imitation model provides no account of how the child might solve these categorisation problems.

We may consider the imitation model as an empiricist account of syntax learning based on the linguistic input to the child from the surrounding environment. An alternative account of the child's early syntactic knowledge may be found in the nativist school of thought; namely, that the child inherits syntax as part of his genetic endowment. The word-order rules described in Brown's schema might be innate. Such an explanation would neatly circumvent the apparent paradox of the imitation model that children learn a set of word-order rules that cannot be found in the adult language. Because the rules are innate, they need not be inferred from the child's linguistic environment. An innate syntactic endowment can be seen as a genetic head-start for the child in the language learning process. Later syntactic acquisitions are a result of the maturation of further syntactic skills as well as an adaptation of existing word-order rules to the syntax of the adult language.

At first glance, the nativist view of syntax acquisition would seem convincing and irrefutable. Brown found no exceptions in children's word-ordering to those predicted by his schema; precisely what one would expect if the knowledge is innate. The further observation that early syntactic structures are only a small subset of those found in the child's linguistic environment further strengthens the nativist hypothesis. However, the view that knowledge of word-order rules in the two-word period is innate gives rise to a number of other predictions, some of which are doubtful, others completely wrong.

If early syntactic structures are innate we would expect to observe the same kind of word-order rules used by all children in the two-word period, irrespective of their native language. Even languages, which in the adult form tend not to use syntax as a means for signalling the meaning relations between the words in the utterance, e.g. Finnish, Hungarian and Russian, should have a developmental stage of two-word utterances in which innate syntactic knowledge manifests itself. Brown's postulation of an Agent-Action-Object-Location schema was based on his observation of three American-English children. What of other languages and cultures? For example, do Finnish or Russian children conform to Brown's schema even though adult users of the language do not? And what of other languages which use syntax to signal meaning relations but use a different syntax from English, e.g. Japanese in which the canonical form is Subject-Object-Action? If word-order rules are innate, then all these children should conform to Brown's schema.

The answer to all these questions is a clear "No!" Once we start observing young children from other cultures, the notion that there is a universal sequencing of words in the two-word period, breaks down. Studies of Finnish, Russian, Korean and German children all indicate alternative word-orders in their utterances. For example, Bowerman (1973) found Finnish children placing the object before the verb in both two- and three-word utterances. This is not the kind of data for supporting a nativist position. An additional problem for the nativist approach concerns the case roles which are the object of the word-order rules. If the child is supposed to have an innate knowledge of the rules for combining agents, actions, objects and locations then one would expect the child to have an innate knowledge of the case roles themselves. This is, of course, parallel to Fillmore's claim that his cases are innate. We have seen that such a claim is questionable, at least as far as the factitive and instrumental cases are concerned (see p. 119). A nativist perspective on the emergence of case roles in children's speech would need to provide a good justification as to why some case roles mature before others.

Both a pure empiricist approach and an untempered nativist hypothesis fail to give us a satisfactory account of the origins of syntax. Across cultures, the variability of the syntactic rules used by children in the two-word stage, defies explanation in terms of universal, innate syntactic knowledge. Within cultures, the discrepancy between the adult model and the child's imitations questions the validity of an environmental, empiricist account based solely on the linguistic input to the child. Unable to use these two traditional explanations of human knowledge and learning, where should we next look for an explanation of the acquisition of syntax?

7.2 Cognitive Development and Syntax Acquisition

So far in this book, we have seen how the study of child language shifted from purely abstract distributional analyses of word-order structures to a description of the meaning relations and the devices for indicating these relations in children's utterances. This shift is best characterised as an attempt to take into account the meaning and context of child language. When we claim that a child is expressing a meaning relation in a two-word utterance, one of our fundamental assumptions is that the child is aware of the relation between the two objects or events described by the words. However, in order to be aware of this relation the child must have developed the cognitive skills necessary for such a conceptualisation. It would be foolish to describe the child as expressing a meaning relation of which he could not yet conceive. Put another way, if we view language as a medium for expressing and representing ideas and thoughts, we should not attribute to the child the linguistic expression of an idea he has not yet mastered.

The Piagetian account of cognitive development argues that language builds upon the foundations of the child's cognitive skills. Particular uses of language must await the appropriate cognitive developments. For example, we have already discussed in chapter two the development of the concept of object permanence. If the child cannot conceive of objects in their absence then we would not expect him to talk about things that were not present in his environment. Indeed, one of the most striking characteristics of early child language is that it always seems to refer to objects and events that can be perceived by the child in the here and now.

Sinclair (1971) has summarised the claim of those who consider cognitive development to be the best perspective for understanding the child's language development.

> Our contention would be (a) that the infant brings to his language acquisition task not a set of innate linguistic universals, but innate cognitive functions which will ultimately result in universal structures of thought; (b) that linguistic universals exist precisely **because** of the universal thought structures – and these are universal, not because they are inborn but because they are the necessary outcome of auto-regulatory factors and equilibration processes;[6] (c) that since intelligence exists phylogenetically and ontogenetically before language, and since the acquisition of linguistic structures is a cognitive activity, cognitive structures should be used to explain language acquisition rather then vice versa. (Sinclair, 1971, p. 123).

Contention (c) essentially denies the plausibility of the Whorf Hypothesis (see chapter two) and argues that linguistic structures can be explained in terms of cognitive structures.

---

6 . By auto-regulatory factors and equilibration processes, Sinclair eludes to Piaget's idea that cognitive development proceeds **not** according to an innate pre-programmed pattern but through an **interaction** of innate predispositions and environmental factors. This interaction is regulated by a process of equilibration which ensures that all individuals go through a universal sequence of development.

Preliminary Approaches to Language Development

Sinclair goes on to give some more concrete arguments as to how cognitive structures might be used to explain emerging linguistic structures. For example, she points out that during the sensorimotor period the child learns to classify objects and events in the course of his activities. The child, in his play with toys, might discover that the same object can be used to perform different actions. Thus, the object can be dissociated from the actions themselves and the object conceptualised as a distinct component of an ongoing event. In contrast, the child will also experience in his play activities the performance of a particular action by different objects, e.g. using various objects to push off the side of a table. In this way, the action can be dissociated from the objects, and the action itself conceptualised as a distinct component of the ongoing event. Instead of perceiving an event as a single unanalysable whole, the child learns to abstract the components parts of the event, objects and actions, through his sensorimotor activities in the world. The ability to abstract, to analyse an event in such a manner indicates that the child is beginning to construct categories for classifying the world. The distinction object/action is perhaps one of the most fundamental classifications that the child learns.

Once the child has developed a category of objects as distinct from actions through his activity in the world, he may begin to notice that objects can play different roles in his activities. For example, an object may be the recipient of some kind of hitting or throwing action by the child, or alternatively the object may be used as an instrument in the process of hitting or reaching for another object. Similarly, the child may discover that people, like objects, can change their role in the performance of an activity. An adult may play the role of both giver and receiver in a giving and taking situation with the child. Whether we consider objects or people, once the child has learnt to analyse events in terms of actions and objects, he will be able to take the further step of identifying the different roles that objects can play in events. Through his practical experiences, the child may even sub-classify the object category into those objects which can instigate an action and those which cannot, e.g. animate vs. inanimate objects.

Clearly, on a purely practical level the child has plenty of opportunity to learn ways of classifying actions, objects and events in the world. This learning constitutes an important part of his cognitive development. In distinguishing objects from actions and learning the different roles that objects can play in relation to various activities, the young child is already learning about aspects of the world which are closely related to the case roles defined in Fillmore's case grammar. For example, in learning to distinguish givers from receivers the child is essentially learning the agentive/dative case distinction. On the other hand, in learning to distinguish an object being hit from using it to hit another object the child could be said to be acquiring the objective/instrumentive case distinction. Through similar experiences the child might learn to identify other case categories like the locative and how to distinguish say the agentive case from the objective case.

The important point is that we need not appeal to innate knowledge to explain the ubiquitous nature of the different case roles. Fillmore's cases are the type of categorical entities that young children will learn during the course of their day-to-day activities in the world (Edwards, 1973). Initially, these categories will exist only on a practical activity level for the infant. But once the practical categories have been formulated, they provide a foundation for the linguistic categories of case grammar. What the infant has achieved on a practical, cognitive level, the young child can later recapitulate on a linguistic level of representation.

Cromer (1974) has called this approach to the study of language development, the **Cognition Hypothesis**. It is a powerful tool for explaining how children might learn the case roles expressed in their early language. However, Sinclair has claimed that cognitive structures can be used to explain the emergence of linguistic structures in general. How then can the cognition hypothesis be used to explain word-order rules in children's language? Sinclair argues that syntactic structures also have their correlates in cognitive structure. She points out that the child's practical activities in the world are not random events but can be described in terms of specific structures. As the child learns to analyse events into their component parts, he also becomes aware of the relations between those component parts. For example, he may come to notice that events have a characteristic agent-action-object structure and may even come to anticipate the participation of each of the component parts of the structure in an event. Sinclair suggests that these **event structures** may form the basis of the child's syntactic knowledge. Just as he perceives the relations between the different components of an event structure, so may the child learn the importance of combining words in an utterance to signal the relations between different parts of the message. Event structures are the cognitive foundations which give rise to the child combining words in his utterances and hence the acquisition of syntactic rules.

Unfortunately, this appealing explanation is difficult to take seriously as a model of syntax acquisition. We have already considered several pieces of evidence that indicate its inadequacy. To begin with, even though the child may indeed be prompted to formulate multi-word utterances in order to encode the different relations in an underlying event structure, Sinclair's model provides us with no description or explanation of the actual syntactic rules that the child uses in the formulation of multi-word utterances. Event structures do not tell the child anything about where, say, the agent or object roles should appear in his utterances. And if they did, we would have the same problem that the nativist hypothesis has in explaining the variability of syntactic rules in early language, across cultures. For the kind of experiences that Sinclair describes as giving rise to these event structures are surely universal and not culture bound. It is difficult to imagine that a Japanese infant does not have the same kind of experience of objects and actions as a Swiss or an English infant. Yet Japanese children use different syntactic rules in their early utterances from Swiss or English children. The cognition hypothesis seems to provide us with a good explanation of how the child comes to talk about agents, actions, objects, locations, etc. and maybe even why he is motivated to combine these categories into multi-word utterances. However, it does not explain the acquisition of syntactic structures themselves.

In our discussion of Brown's propositional schema, we saw how it was important to distinguish between a purely conceptual analysis of an event and a linguistic representation of that event e.g. a propositional structure. I argued that word-order rules and evidence for the existence of case frames in two-word utterances could support the postulation of an underlying, intermediate propositional structure as distinct from a non-linguistic conceptual structure. To construct propositional structures the child must undoubtedly have an even deeper conceptual representation of the intended message. However, word-order rules operate at the level of linguistic (i.e. propositional) structure. To appeal to an underlying conceptual structure for an explanation of their existence would obliterate the need for an intermediate level of linguistic representation. A consequence of such an obliteration would be the prediction that early syntactic structures are the same across all languages – a prediction which we have seen to be false. Not only must we accept the need for an intermediate level of linguistic representation of our ideas and thoughts but we must look elsewhere than conceptual, event structures for an explanation of the origins of syntax.

7.3   An Interactional Model of Syntax Acquisition.

Macnamara (1972) has put forward a model of syntax acquisition which combines aspects of the empiricist, linguistic input approach with that of the cognitive developmentalist's. He stresses the need to take into account the variety of syntactic structures both within and across languages but points out that however abstract word-order rules may be, they are basically devices for signalling meaning relations. These meaning relations should match up to what we know about the child's cognitive development.

Macnamara begins his argument with the proposal that the young child's learning of syntax might be guided by a single underlying principle. For example, the child might assume that a single semantic relation is always signalled by means of a single syntactic device and that any change in syntactic structure signals a change in semantic structure. However, as Macnamara points out, identical semantic structures may be signalled by quite different syntactic structures. Sentence pairs 7.1.) and 7.2.) are examples of two sentences which have precisely the same meaning yet different word-order structures.

> 7.1. a) Give the book to me.
>   b) Give me the book.
> 7.2. a) My hair is black.
>   b) I have black hair.

The difference in syntactic structures between the sentences in each pair does not signal a change in semantic structure. Rather, the differences involved would appear to be more associated with a person's **style** of speaking. In contrast, a single syntactic structure can also be used to indicate a diverse range of semantic structures. The prepositional phrases 7.3.), 7.4.), and 7.5.) suggest quite different meaning relations between the preposition "in" and its

    7.3.)   In a minute.

    7.4.)   In a box.

    7.5.)   In a temper.

associated noun phrases even though the syntactic structures of these prepositional phrases are identical. Clearly, a child who adopted the principle of a one-to-one mapping of syntactic structures onto semantic structures would not get very far in the process of syntax acquisition.

However, suppose that the child has discovered that sentences 7.1a) and 7.1b) are only stylistic variants of each other. How is he then to conclude that sentences 7.6.) and 7.7.) have different semantic structures and are not stylistic variants like 7.1) and 7.1b)? The syntactic diversity between sentences 7.1a) and 7.1b) is greater than that between sentences 7.6.) and 7.7.).

    7.6.)   The boy is hitting the girl.

    7.7.)   The girl is hitting the boy.

Macnamara argues that, "There is in fact no way to decide the matter unless one has independent access to the meaning, probably through observing what is happening at the time such sentences are uttered" (Macnamara, 1972, p. 6). In other words, it is impossible to discover the syntactic structures relevant to a particular language without a knowledge of the meaning that those structures are supposed to convey. A young child could not know that sentences 7.6.) and 7.7.) had different meanings whilst 7.1a) and 7.1b) had the same meaning, unless he had alternative sources of information about the sentences' semantic structures. As Macnamara points out, this alternative source of information is likely to be the child's perception of the situation in which the utterance is produced. Thus sentence 7.6.) is uttered in a situational context different from that of sentence 7.7.). Sentences 7.1a) and 7.1b) might well be uttered in identical contexts.

Macnamara's model of syntax acquisition views the child as using meaning as the key to a language's word-order rules. The child relates the utterance to the ongoing context and then uses his understanding of the context to "figure out" what the syntactic rules of the language must be. For example, we may imagine an adult uttering sentence 7.6.) to a child whilst both are watching a quarrel or whilst looking through a picture book. In this situation the child can construct a conceptual representation of the event through a combination of his perceptual skills and his knowledge of event structures of the type described by Sinclair above. If we assume that the child realises the adult's utterance is of relevance to this conceptual representation, we can begin to see how the child might decipher the syntactic structures of his language. He will be able to "figure out" that the person doing the the hitting is the first person mentioned in the sentence whilst the person being hit is mentioned last. If the event structure changes so that the girl starts hitting the boy, the adult might then produce sentence 7.7.). Again the child will be able to use his knowledge of the event structure to deduce that the first person mentioned in the sentence was doing the hitting and so on. Furthermore, the contrast between sentences 7.6.) and 7.7) and their respective event structures will lead the child to an understanding that such changes in word-order are important in signalling changes in meaning. In a similar way, the child can discover that sentences 7.1a) and 7.1b) are only stylistic variants of each other.

This approach to describing the learning of syntax can account for most of the syntactic devices that a child must learn in order to signal the important meaning relations in his language. In effect, the child has to be on the lookout for changes in syntactic structure whenever there is a change in the event structure. Any observed syntactic changes then become candidate devices for signalling the conceived change in the event structure. When event structure changes involve role reversals, as in sentences 7.6.) and 7.7.), syntax learning will be especially effective because it directly reveals a word-order device of the language. Indeed, one might even predict that progress in syntax learning is most likely to occur in those situations where the adult produces utterance combinations like 7.6.) and 7.7.) in response to changes in the event structure. Providing such combinations, may be one way in which the adult can help the child come to an understanding of the syntactic structures of his language. Macnamara's proposal, thus relates syntax acquisition to the child's developing conceptual structures and the syntactic structures used by adult speakers of his native language. The origins of syntax can be found in the interaction between these conceptual and linguistic representations; an interaction motivated by the child's own willingness to learn his nature tongue.

This model of syntax acquisition is probably the best available today. However, it assumes a number of skills and activities on be-half of the child that are themselves problematic in nature. For ex-ample, how does the child relate the different components of his event structure to the utterance of the adult? How does the child discover which part of the sentence maps onto the relevant part of the event structure? If he could not map the noun phrases "The boy" and "The girl" in sentences 7.6.) and 7.7.) onto the correct compo-nents in their respective event structures, the child would be unable to decipher the appropriate word-order rules. One obvious criterion for successfully performing this mapping procedure is that the child knows the meaning of phrases or words like "Boy" and "Girl". Be-cause the child knows the meaning of these words, he can quickly identify which parts of the sentence map onto the different compo-nents of the event structure. In this way, knowledge of **word mean-ing** becomes a prerequisite for the acquisition of syntax through its determination of the mapping process.

However, even knowledge of word meaning is not enough for the learning process to proceed smoothly. The child must also be aware of the simple fact that the words in the adult's utterances have a particular order and that this order can change, as in sentences 7.6.) and 7.7.). Recognising the words in the sentence will of course facilitate the awareness of order. Nevertheless, the child still needs some tool for encoding word-order in a sentence and comparing it with subsequent orderings. The child must be sensitive to the fact that word-order is an important aspect of linguistic knowledge. This sensivity may take the form of innate linguistic knowledge such as that proposed by Chomsky. Alternatively, a general perceptual me-chanism which directs the child to attend to the order of his per-ceptions might fulfil this function equally well.

Finally, we must ask the question as to what motivates the child to assume that the adult utterance relates to some aspect of the ongoing situation. What prompts the child to believe that event structures and linguistic structures might be linked? At an even deeper level, what prompts the child to assume that language is worth learning in the first place? All of these issues - word mean-ing, order perception and motivation - are problems that need to be solved if Macnamara's model of syntax acquisition is to work.

140

7.4 Concluding Remarks

We have witnessed a gradual shift from highly abstract linguistic accounts of language development to more conceptually based approaches to the language learning process. This shift reflected a growing trend in the seventies for researchers to focus on non-linguistic factors in the process of language development. The child does not learn to speak just for the sake of learning a language but in the context of his many and diverse activities. In this respect, the Piagetian tradition of describing development came to have a strong influence on child language theories. You will recall from chapter two that Piaget considered language to be secondary to thought in the developmental process. Child language research in the seventies also tended to take this view through attempts to explain language development in terms of other underlying non-linguistic skills. However, as we have seen in this chapter, these attempts could not be entirely successful because of the diversity of linguistic skills both across and within cultures. Non-linguistic explanations of language development tend to predict the existence of universal features after the fashion of the nativist hypothesis.

In a number of respects, the learning of a language must depend on the language itself. No amount of cognitive development is going to inform the French child that a dog is called "un chien" rather than "un dog". Neither could the Japanese child similarly discover that the canonical sentence form of his language is SOV. The problem for the child language researcher is to identify those aspects of linguistic knowledge which are specifically linguistic, i.e. cannot be explained in terms of other non-linguistic structure. The need for a linguistic level of representation of utterances over and above a purely conceptual level of representation highlights the importance of distinguishing linguistic and non-linguistic factors and the relation between them, in the process of language development.

BIBLIOGRAPHY

Bloom, L. (1970). Language development: Form and function in emerging grammars. Cambridge, Mass.: M.I.T. Press.

Bloom, L. (1973). One word at a time. The Hague: Mouton.

Boulding, K.E. (1956). The Image. Ann Arbor: University of Michigan Press.

Bowerman, M. (1973). Early Syntactic Development: A Cross-Linguistic Study with Special Reference to Finnish. Cambridge: Cambridge University Press.

Bowerman, M. (1978). The Acquisition of Word Meaning: An Investigation into some Current Conflicts. In N. Waterson & C. Snow (eds.). The Development of Communication. New York: Wiley.

Braine, M.D.S. (1963). The ontogeny of English phrase structure: The first phrase: Language, 39, 1-13.

Brown, G. & Desforges, C. (1979). Piaget's Theory. A psychological critique. Routledge & Kegan Paul. London.

Brown, R. (1973). A first language: The early stages. Cambridge, Mass.: Harvard University Press.

Brown, R. & Bellugi, U. (1964). Three processes in the child's acquisition of syntax. Harvard Educational Review, 34, 133-151.

Carroll, J.B. & Casagrande, J.B. (1958). "The function of language classifications in behaviour", in Maccoby, E.E., Newcomb, T.M. and Hartley, E.L. (eds.) Readings in social psychology (3rd edition). New York: Holt, Rinehart and Winston.

Chomsky, N. (1957). Syntactic Structures. The Hague: Mouton.

Clark, E.V. (1973). What's in a word? On the child's acquisition of semantics in his first language. In T.E. Moore (ed.), Cognitive development and the acquisition of language. New York: Academic Press.

Corrigan, R.A. (1978). Language development as related to stage 6 object permanence development. Journal of Child Language, 5, 173-189.

143

Cromer, R.F. (1974). The development of language and cognition: the cognition hypothesis. In B. Foss (ed.), New Perspectives in Child Development. Harmondsworth: Penguin.

Edwards, D. (1973). Sensori-motor intelligence and semantic relations in early child grammar. Cognition, 2, 395-434.

Fillmore, C.J. (1968). The case for case. In E. Bach & R.T. Harms (eds.), Universals in linguistic theory. New York: Holt, Rinehart & Winston.

Garret, M.F., Bever, T.G., and Fodor, J.A. The active use of grammar in speech perception. Perception and Psychophysics. 1, 30-32.

Halliday, M.A.K. (1975). Learning How to Mean: explorations in the development of language. London: Edward Arnold.

Johnson, N.F. (1965). The psychological reality of phrase structure rules. Journal of Verbal Learning and Verbal Behaviour. 4. pp. 469-475.

Kohler, W. (1925). The Mentality of Apes. Translated by E. Winter. London: Kegan Paul.

Macnamara, J. (1972). Cognitive basis of language Learning in infants. Psychological Review, 79, 1-13.

McNeill, D. (1970). The Acquisition of Language: the study of developmental psycholinguistics. New York: Harper & Row.

McShane, J. (1979). The development of naming. Linguistics, 17, 879-905.

McShane, J. & Whittaker, S. (1982). The role of symbolic thought in language development. Paper presented at the "Acquisition Of Symbolic Skills" Conference, University of Keele, July 1982.

Miller, G.A. (1962). Some psychological studies of grammar. American Psychologist, 17, pp. 748-762.

Nelson, K. (1973). Structure and strategy in learning to talk. Monographs of the Society for Research in Child Development, 38, (1-2, Serial No. 149).

Piaget, J. (1926). The language and thought of the child. New York: Harcourt, Brace & Jovanovich.

Piaget, J. (1945). Play, dreams and imitation in childhood. Translated by C. Cattegno and F.M. Hodgson. London: Routledge & Kegan Paul, 1951.

Plunkett, K. (1985). Om referencefunktionens ontogenese. (On Learning How to Refer). Nordisk Psykolog, 37.

144

Rosch, E. & Mervis, C.B. (1975). Family resemblance studies in the internal structure of categories. Cognitive Psychology, 7, 573–605.

Schlesinger, I.M. (1977). The role of cognitive development and linguistic input in language acquisition. Journal of Child Language, 4, 153–169.

Sinclair, H. (1971). Sensorimotor Action Patterns as a Condition for the Acquisition of Syntax. In R. Huxley & E. Ingram (eds.), Language Acquisition: Models and Methods. London: Academic Press.

Slobin, D.I. (1966). Grammatical transformations and sentence comprehension in childhood and adulthood. Journal of Verbal Learning and Verbal Behaviour, 5, pp. 219–227.

Slobin, D.I. (1970). Universals of grammatical development in children. In G.B. Flores d'Arcais & W.J.M. Levelt (eds.), Advances in Psycholinguistics. Amsterdam: North Holland Publishing Company.

Uzgiriz, I.C. & Hunt, J.McV. (1975). Assessment in Infancy. Chicago: University of Illinois Press.

Vygotsky, L. (1962). Thought and Language. Cambridge, Mass.: M.I.T. Press.

Whorf, B.L. (1956). Language, thought and reality: selected writings of Benjamin Lee Whorf. (Edited by Carroll, J.B.). New York: M.I.T. Press & Wiley.

INDEX

Action: pp. 9, 18, 20-22
Action-location: p. 117
Action-object: p. 102
Actor: p. 9
Adjective: pp. 58, 63, 66, 88
Adverb: p. 58
Agent-action: p. 102
Agent-object: p. 99, 102, 104
Agentive case: pp. 110, 126
Ambiguous: pp. 58, 66, 67, 72
Ambiguity: pp. 66, 67, 72
Animate nouns: pp. 93, 94
Anthropology: pp. 55, 60
Associative complexes: pp. 28, 29
Attention: p. 45
Attribute-entity: pp. 117, 118
Attributes: pp. 10, 27-29
Attributive: pp. 93, 97

Babbling: p. 98
Behavourist: pp. 15, 16, 38, 39
Bellugi, U.: p. 91
Bever, T.G.: p. 64
Bloom, L.: pp. 35, 50, 91-95, 97-99, 101-104, 119, 122, 124
Boulding, K.E.: p. 14
Bowerman, M.: pp. 26, 88, 132
Braine, M.D.S.: pp. 85, 86, 88-90, 125
Branching(s): pp. 56, 63
Brown: R.: pp. 91, 102, 103, 116-118, 120, 123, 124, 126, 127, 129, 130, 131, 136

Canonical form: pp. 129, 131

Carrol, J.B.: pp. 10–12

Case frame: pp. 110, 112, 113, 115, 116,, 119–122, 126–128

Case grammar: pp. 105, 109–111, 114–124, 126

Case marker: pp. 111, 113–115

Case relation(s): pp. 108–110, 112–114, 116, 120

Cassagrande, J.B.: pp. 10–12

Chomsky, N.: pp. 55, 60, 61, 66–69, 72, 73, 76–83, 92, 94, 98, 99, 101, 103, 107, 108, 130, 140

Clark, E.V. p. 31

Click: pp. 64, 65

Cognition hypothesis: pp. 135, 136

Cognitive determination: pp. 9, 10, 12, 13, 17, 23, 29

Cognitive development: pp. 132–134, 137, 141

Collection: p. 29

Common name: p. 33

Communication: p. 43

Comparative linguist: p. 7

Complexes: pp. 28, 29

Comprehension: p. 31

Concept: p. 14, 19–22, 26–29

Concept formation: pp. 26–29

Conceptual representation: pp. 136, 139

Context: pp. 81, 83, 89–92, 98, 103, 104

Conversation: pp. 38, 43, 44

Conversational: pp. 38, 43

Corrigan, R.A.: pp. 36–38, 48–51

Cromer, R.F.: p. 135

Dative case: pp. 110, 113, 116, 117, 120–122, 126

Dative–objective: pp. 117, 118, 120

Deaf children: p. 34

Decalage: p. 51

Deep structure: pp. 69–75

Demonstratives: p. 88

Demonstrative–entity: pp. 117, 118

Derivational theory of complexity (DTC): p. 74

Dialogue: pp. 39–44, 47

Differentiation: pp. 87, 88
Distributional(ly): p. 68
Distributional analysis: pp. 90–92

Edwards, D.: p. 135
Empiricist: pp. 130, 132, 137
English: pp. 10–12
Entity-location: pp. 117, 118
Equilibration: p. 133
Error(s): pp. 62, 63
Event structures: pp. 135–137, 139, 140
Evolution: p. 18
Expansions: pp. 90–92, 94
Experimental background: p. 12
Experimental psychology: pp. 10
Experimental variable: p. 13
Explanatory function: p. 61

Factitive case: p. 119
Fillmore, C.J.: pp. 107–119, 121, 132, 135
Final pivot: pp. 85–88
Finnish: p. 88
Fodor, J.A.: p. 64
Frequency: p. 84
Function word: p. 46

Garret, M.F.: pp. 64–66, 73
Genitive: p. 117
Gestural: p. 41
Gesture: pp. 42, 46
Grammatical categories: pp. 58, 59, 68

Halliday, M.A.K.: p. 47
Hebrew: p. 7
Here and now: pp. 18, 19, 22
Hierarchical structure: p. 56
Hunt, J.McV.: p. 36

Idealism: p. 34
Imitating: pp. 34, 43, 44
Imitation: pp. 37, 44
Imperative: p. 71
India: p. 7
Inflection: pp. 80, 105, 106, 111, 114, 115
Initial pivot: pp. 85, 86, 90
Innate knowledge: pp. 79, 80, 98
Insight: pp. 44, 47, 48, 53
Instruction: p. 14
Instrumental pp. 46, 47, 50
Instrumental case: pp. 105, 107, 108, 109, 111, 112, 114, 115, 119
Instrumental function: p. 45
Interactionist: p. 16
Interrogative: pp. 71, 73
Intuitions: pp. 66, 67, 69, 72
Invisible displacement: p. 21
Irregular forms: pp. 81, 82
Irreversible passives: p. 100

Japanese: p. 7
Johnson, N.F.: pp. 61-64, 66, 73
Joint attention: pp. 43, 44, 47

Knowing how: pp. 14, 22
Knowing that: p. 14
Knowledge: pp. 13-15, 17, 22, 26
Kohler, W.: p. 48

Language Acquisition Device (LAD): pp. 98, 99
Learnability: p. 77
Lexical rules: p. 57
Lexicon feature rules: pp. 93, 94
Linguistic categorisation: pp. 10
Linguistic competence: pp. 61, 66, 67
Linguistic determinism, p. 9
Linguistic input: pp. 130, 132, 137
Linguistic relativity: pp. 8, 9
Linguistic skills: p. 43

Linquistic structures: p. 9
Linguistic universals: p. 133
Literal translation: p. 9
Locative case: pp. 110, 111, 120, 124, 126, 127
Longitudinal data: p. 43

Macnamara, J.: pp. 137-140
Maturation: pp. 15-17, 23
McNeill, D.: pp. 87, 88
McShane, J.: pp. 45, 47, 49, 50, 52, 53
Meaning relations: pp. 95, 97, 99, 102, 103
Memory limitation: p. 95
Mental image: p. 48
Methodological problems: p. 13
Middle-class: p. 11
Miller, G.A. pp. 74-76
Modality: pp. 109, 115
Morpheme: pp. 81, 82
Morphemic rule: p. 82

Names: pp. 8, 9, 27, 29, 31-36, 39-41, 43, 44, 46, 47, 52, 53
Naming: pp. 31-44, 46-54
Nativist: pp. 131, 132, 136, 141
Navajo: pp. 10-12
Negation: p. 71
Negative: pp. 71, 73, 75
Nelson, K.: p. 47
Node(s): pp. 56-60, 63, 68
Noun: pp. 56, 58, 59, 68
Noun phrase: pp. 56, 58-60, 63, 67, 68, 70

Object: pp. 9-11, 14, 15, 17-22, 27-29
Object permanence: pp. 19-23, 34-38, 46, 48-54
Object-word mapping: p. 52
Objective case: pp. 110, 112, 113, 115, 120, 121, 123, 124, 127, 128
Open class: pp. 85-88, 92
Optional rules: pp. 93-95
Overgeneralisation: p. 82

Passive: pp. 69, 70, 73, 75

Past tense: pp. 81, 82

Performance: pp. 78, 95, 96

Phonetic: pp. 32, 34, 35, 40

Phrase structure (grammar): pp. 55, 58–64

Piaget, J.: pp. 15–18, 20, 22, 23, 25, 34, 35, 48–52, 133, 141

Picture evaluation task: p. 99

Pivot class: pp. 85–88

Placement transformation: p. 93

Plural: pp. 81, 82

Possession: pp. 92, 99

Possessor-possessed: pp. 92, 93, 97, 104

Pragmatic rule: p. 82

Pre-intellectual phase: p. 25

Pre-linguistic phase: p. 25

Preposition: pp.58, 88

Prepositional phrase(s): p. 63

Pre-school child: p. 16

Present participle: p. 66

Principle of irreversibility: p. 16

Productivity: pp. 81, 86, 89

Pronouns: pp. 38, 58, 88

Proposition: pp. 109, 110, 112, 113, 115–117, 120–123, 126

Propositional structure: pp. 110, 112, 115, 116, 120–128

Proper name: p. 33

Psycholinguistics: p. 74

Psychological reality: pp. 64, 65, 73, 76

Recall: p. 19

Recognition: p. 19

Reduction transformation: p. 93

Referent: pp. 48, 49

Referring: pp. 33, 34, 38

Representation: pp. 13, 19, 21, 22

Request: pp. 41, 42

Reversible passives: p. 101

Ritual naming game: pp. 47, 52

Rosch, E.: p. 29

Rote learning: p. 77

Rule(s): pp. 55–63, 68–73

Rule 3: p. 109

Rule 5: pp. 112, 113

Schlesinger, I.M. p. 9

Self–reflection: p. 23

Semantic interpretation: p. 104

Semantic knowledge: p. 68

Semantic representation: pp. 115, 121

Sensorimotor period: pp. 17, 18, 35, 48

Sentence: pp. 55–57, 59–63, 65–69, 71–76

Sentence complexity: pp. 73, 74

Shape: pp. 10–12, 15, 26–28

Sign: pp. 34, 46, 47

Sign language: p. 34

Simple active sentence: pp. 69–71

Sinclair, H.: pp. 133–136, 139

Single–word utterance: pp. 83, 85, 98

Singular: p. 82

Social function: p. 25

Socialisation: p. 26

Sociocultural experience: pp. 23, 24

Stage 4 error: p. 20

Stage 4: pp. 37, 46

Stage 5: pp. 21, 37

Stage 6: pp. 21, 35–37, 50, 51

Statement: p. 41

Structural description: pp. 55, 61, 66, 67, 69

Structural differences: pp. 8, 17, 24

Structural relation(s): pp. 60, 61

Structuralist: pp. 15, 16

Style: p. 137

Stylistic variant: pp. 138, 139

Subject: p. 9

Subject–locative: pp. 93, 97

Subject–object: pp. 92, 93, 96, 97

Substantive form: p. 50

Surface structure: pp. 67, 69–74, 76

Symbol: pp. 18, 48–50, 52, 53

Symbolic capacity: pp. 18, 19, 21, 25, 48–52, 54
Symbolic representation: pp. 19, 22, 48, 51
Symbolic skill: pp. 8, 17, 18, 22, 23, 48, 52, 53, 54
Syntactic rules: p. 69
Syntax: pp. 78, 80

Terminal elements: pp. 58, 60
Terminal string: pp. 96, 97
Transformational grammar: pp. 55, 66, 68, 69, 72, 73, 76
Transformational rule: pp. 70–73
Transformational tag: pp. 70, 71
Transition Error Probability (TEP): pp. 62–64
Tree diagrams: pp. 56, 57, 62
Trial-and-error: pp. 15, 28
Two-word (utterance): pp. 83–90, 101–104

Universal: pp. 77, 79, 80, 98, 99
Universal grammar: pp. 77, 79, 80, 98
Uzgiris, I.C.: p. 36

Verb: pp. 9, 10, 24
Verb (auxiliary): pp. 56–60, 63, 66
Verb phrase: pp. 56, 58–60, 63, 67, 68, 70
Verbal thought: p. 24
Vocabulary: pp. 31, 36, 38, 44–52
Vocabulary growth: pp. 31, 36, 44, 46
Vygotsky, L.: pp. 23–29
Vygotsky's blocks: p. 26

Well-formedness: p. 90
Whorf, B.L.: pp. 7–13, 23–25, 29, 133
Whorf Hypothesis: pp. 7–13, 23, 24, 29
Word meaning: pp. 24–29, 140
Word-order rules: pp. 9
Word-order schema: pp. 124–125